*J. R. Thompson.*

# Travellers Guide

# to

# Albania

*Every effort is made to ensure accuracy, but the publishers do not hold themselves responsible for any consequences that may arise from errors or omissions. Whilst the contents are believed to be correct at the time of going to press, changes may have occurred since that time or will occur during the currency of this book.*

*All rights reserved. No part of this publication may be reproduced, stored in a retrieval system, or transmitted in any form or by means - electronic, mechanical, photocopying, recording or otherwise - unless the written permission of the Publisher has been given beforehand.*

Written by        Agim Neza and Miranda Hanka
Edited by         Drita Dracini and Andre Axford
Photographs by    Petrit Kenuti

© Copyright ACO UK 1993 First Edition
ISBN 0-9521573-0-6

"History has been cruel to us, but neither did we appear sad, fearful or defeated. We exude a strength of character forged by years of coping with hard struggles to preserve our liberty, our mother tongue and our culture"

Agim Neza

Contents

I. Country Profile

- Geographical Survey

- National symbols and feasts

- Historical Chronology

II. Itinerary One - Central Region

III. Itinerary Two - Southern Region

IV. Itinerary Three - Nothern Region

V. Tirana Business Digest

VI. Bibliography

VII. Literature

VIII. Vocabulary

# COUNTRY PROFILE

*Geographic Position*

Albania is situated on the western part of the Balkan peninsula between 39 38' and 42 39', northern geographic latitudes 19 16' and 21 4' eastern geographic longitudes.

Albania borders with Yugoslavia on the northeast, Greece on the southeast, whereas in the west it borders with the Adriatic and Ionian seas. Its total land surfaces 28,748 km. The total length of its boundary line is 1,204 km, of which, 544 km are land boundaries, 472 are sea and 155 km are lake and river boundaries.

*Landscape*

It is mainly a mountainous country. More than two thirds of the territory is made up of hills and mountains, whereas the plains, with an altitude of upto 200 m above sea level comprise the remainder. The average altitude of the country is 714 m above sea level.

Because of the innumerable valleys that intersect the mountain ranges and of a series of depressed areas sunken deep between the mountains, the relief is highly accentuated with a large number of small hills that form landscapes and sceneries of rare beauty and therefore of great touristic value. These small hills are closely interwoven with one another to form larger mountain ranges, quite distinct from one another:- The Alps of north Albania; - The Central mountain range; - The Southern mountain region; - The Western lowlands.

*- The Alps of Northern Albania.*
These mountains are situated along the right side of the Drin valley. On the whole, their average altitude is 1,500m above sea level, however the greater part of them exceeds 2,000 m, with the highest peak being Jezerca at 2,693 m above sea level. The form of the region is very rugged, with pyramid-like mountains full of deep ravines and valleys which make them look higher than they actually are. The valleys of Boga, Thethi and Jezerca leave an amazing impression on the visitor.

- *The Central Mountain Region.*
These mountains are situated between the valley of Drin and the valleys and rivers Lower Devoll and Upper Osum. They differ from the region of the Northern Alps in that they are not rugged. The general structure of the relief there are three main mountains running from northwest to southeast. The highest peak in this range being Mount Korabi at 2,751m above sea level, which is situated on the eastern-most range. In addition there are two long depressions that stretch between them, Mati and Upper Shkumbini and the depression of Drini i Zi.

The most fascinating part of the region are the lakes of Lura, which are considered to be 'the pearls of Albanian landscape'.

At the southeastern end of the region there is a zone of deeply embedded depression between the mountains, forming large and beautiful lakes of Ohri and Prespa. Amongst the important plains of the region is that of Korca, which occupies a special place in our economy.

- *The Southern Mountain Range.*

These mountains are situated south of the central region and offer a still more regular tectonic structure, characterised by the presence of a series of limestone mountains and valleys running parallel with each other, from northwest to southwest. Most of the mountain peaks are 2,000 m above sea level, however there are some valleys that drop down to sea level. The highest mountains of the region are Tomorri at 2,417 and Papingji at 2,486. The mountains of the southern region are mostly bare or covered with scant forests.

- *Western Depression.*

The Western Depression is situated on the western part of Albania extending along the coast line of the Adriatic sea. It is composed of low altitude plains. Thus differing markedly from the three previous mountain regions. This depression stretches for 200 km from the Lake of Hoti in the North, to Vlore in the south. In the east it extends up to the western slopes of the North Alps, of the Central mountain range and those of the southern mountain range penetrating up to 50 km from the sea shore. A range of hills divide the depression into separate plains. On the whole the plains have a negligible inclination, mostly they do not rise more than 20 metres above sea level. Along the sea shore there are many lagoons and stretches of sand, the later forming ideal bathing beaches such as those of Ahengjin, Durres and Divjake. These are the most densely populated regions of Albania.

*The Climate.*

Albania is situated in a zone with the Mediterranean climate. However, because of the mountainous characteristics of the country and of the very accentuated relief surface, the climate is not the same all over the territory. The meteorological conditions change rapidly from southwest to northwest, the temperatures and the precipitation diminish in this same direction. The amount of rain and snow fall is sufficient (about 1,300mm per annum), but is unevenly distributed during the year. It is concentrated mainly during the cold season and the summer, on the whole, is hot and dry. The average annual temperature increases from northeast at 25'C to southeast 17.5'C. The hottest month is July with an average temperature of 25'C. The highest recorded summer temperature is at Kucova 43.9'C.

The coldest month is January with an average temperature of 6'C. The eastern part of Albania has very cold winters. The lowest recorded temperature being -34'C at the resort of Biza, 35 km east of Tirana.

The winds have a seasonal character, during the cold half of the year and especially during the winter months, the air moves from the land towards the sea reducing the land temperature. The situation is reversed during the summer months.

The peculiarities of the relief have conditioned the existence of certain local winds. thus the most characteristic winter wind is the 'Murlan', a cold, dry and very strong wind. The 'Sirocco' or native 'Juga' wind is a warm, moist oppressive wind laden with rain. In the regions along the sea, predominate cool sea breezes that blow during the months of June, July and August.

Bearing in mind the peculiarities of the climate and the above mentioned distribution of the meteorological elements the western part on Albania, where the softening influence of the sea is felt more and has a much milder winter and a hotter summer. Whereas the interior of the country, where the territorial winds prevail, has quite a severe winter, with more pronounced contrasts in temperature between the winter and the summer months.

*The Hydrography.*

Albania is rich in rivers and streams. The regime of the rivers and streams is torrential with great differences in the amount of water they carry from season to season, a fact that explains their great eroding capacity. The rivers are very important for the irrigation of the land and for the production of hydro electric power. The biggest hydro electric stations are Koman, Fierza and Vau i Dejes. The most important rivers are Drin in the north and Shkumbin and Semen in the south. The Drin river has two springs, one coming from Lake Ohrid and the other from Kosovo. The longest river in Albania is the Semen which is 281 km and is divided into two separate branches, Devoll and Osum. The river Vjosa, 272 km long, originates from the Smolika mountain and is the most torrent in Albania. Other rivers to mention are the Erzen, Mat and Ishem, however the only navigable river is the Buna in the north of the country.

*Flora and Fauna.*

The great climatic, geographic and physical variety of the Albanian territory explains the presence of a rich plant and animal life. Albania has a great variety of plants, representing the greater part of the plant life of the Balkan Peninsula. In general, the flora of the western part of the Albanian territory is represented mainly by the Mediterranean evergreen shrubbery and bushes, whereas in the interior of the land is predominated by the plant life of Central Europe ; broad-leaf trees, like the oak and coniferous trees, but here too Mediterranean varieties are not lacking. The Albanian Alps have typical Alpine flora represented by various grasses and vetch, forming excellent summer grazing grounds for sheep and goats. The flora of Albania is very rich in medicinal plants (juniper berry, sage, jimsom, weed, thyme, linden flowers, squills, salep, mint etc). Rich and multifarious is the animal life, represented by a great variety of wild animals (hares, foxes, weasels, bears, otters, wolves, jackels, wild goats etc) and wild birds (partridges, eagles, turtle-doves, wild cocks, pheasants etc) as well as aquatic birds (wild ducks, wild geese, herons, swans, pelicans etc). The fauna of Albania represents a considerable natural wealth, being a source of game supply and a source of costly skins and furs.

*The Population.*

The population of Albania, after the records of 1986, is 3.2 million. The average density of population, at present, is 103 inhabitants per square km. It is estimated that the population of the present territory of Albania in 1876 was 740,000.

Ethnically, 99% of the population is Albanian, but there is a Greek minority of some 50,000 in the south and southeast, a minority of some 4,000 Macedonians near lake Prespa in the east, and a small number of Vllachs in Central and Southeastern Albania.

65% of the population lives in the countryside, while 35% lives in cities and towns. Albanian's live not only in Albania. Following the Turkish invasion in the fifteenth century, many Albanian's emigrated; today the decedents of these emigrants form the Albanian minority in Calabria and Sicily, known as "Aeberesh". Later, in 1913, the boundaries of the state were arbitrarily drawn by the Great Powers, so as to place some 2 million Albanian's in what became Yugoslavia. There are Albanian's living in Kosovo, Montenegro and Macedonia. There are also Albanian colonies in the U.S.A., Argentina, Australia, Bulgaria, Egypt, Greece, Romania, Turkey, so that the number of ethnic Albanian's in the world totals more than 6 million.

The population is very young - with an average age of 26 years. 40% of the population is under 16 years of age. Life expectancy is 70.4 years (against 38.3 years in 1938).

*The Albanian National Flag;*

The Albanian national flag is red with a black double-headed eagle in the middle. Officially, the flag was confirmed on March 15 1946, however originally adopted from 1912, when the country was proclaimed independent. The symbol of the eagle originates from Scanberbeg's time. During Italian invasion, in 1939, the Albanian's were prohibited to use their national flag. In 1945 a five pointed red star was put above the double-headed eagle, as a symbol of the new socialist state order. The emblem of Scanderbeg also had a star but it was a six-pointed one. The star was situated in the middle of a black track right above the eagle. Recently, with the democratic changes in the country, the star has been taken off the flag.

The Albanian anthem is "Hymni i Flamurit" ("The Anthem of the Flag"), used since 1912, the year of independence. The music was composed in 1880. The text is written by an Albanian writer, Aleksander Stavri Drenova, known as Asdreni (1872-1947).

*The national and popular feasts in Albania;*

| | |
|---|---|
| 1 January | New Year |
| 11 January | Republic Day (1946) |
| 7 March | Teacher's Day |
| 8 March | Mother's Day |
| 12 April | Easter |
| 5 May | Martyr's Day |
| 1 June | Children's Day |
| 28 November | Independence Day (1912) |
| 29 November | Liberation Day (1944) |
| 25 December | Christmas Day |

*Historical chronology of Albania.*

The forerunners of the present day Albanian's were the Illyrians. They inhabited a large territory, ranging from Istria to the Save and the Gulf of Arta, and extending even into Calabria, as early as Middle Palaeolithic (100.000 - 40.000 B.C). But the first considerable traces of civilization are to be found in (6.000 - 2.000 B.C).

Here is a chronology of the historical data ;

B.C 5.000  Palasgians migrate to the Balkans, beginning of the Bronze-age.

B.C 1.000  Illyrians travel from Central Europe to settle in the Western Balkans.

B.C 7/8th  Greeks from Corfu and Corinth, colonies the Albanian coast. Founding of Epidamnos (in B.C 627 as the Greek colony, Dyrrachion - later known as Durres) and Apollonia (B.C 5-3-rd century, flowering of the state of Illyria).

B.C 435  Conflict between the Independent city state of Epidamnos and Corfu.

B.C 250  A state under king Agron controls the Western shores of the Balkans territory from river Krka in Slovenia to the present day Albania.

B.C 229-168  Roman invasion of the Illyrian coast. Illyrian kingdom is reduced to a narrow strip between Dubrovnick and Lezhe. At this time was built the "Via Egnatia" from Dyrrachion (Durres) to Constantinople.

B.C 167  Rome is victorious against King Genthius, bringing his Illyrian kingdom under Roman rule.

| | |
|---|---|
| A.D. 2nd C | Illyrians became known by the new name of Arber Christianity spreads. |
| A.D. 160-927 | Slavonic tribes occupy the mountain districts of Albania. |
| A.D. 395 | Arberia becomes part of the Byzantine Empire. |
| A.D. 5th C | Invasion by western and eastern Goths, Avars and Celts. They ravage the Balkan provinces, stay a short time, then move on, Huns invade Kosovo. |
| 529 - 640 | Invasion from central Europe by Slavic tribes ending Byzantine authority. The Illyrian population withdraws into the coastal towns and the mountains of the interior of northern Albania. |
| 851 | Invasion of the area by the Bulgars, who stay until C. 1010. |
| 1054 | Schism in the church - division into Orthodox and Roman churches. Schism effects Albania's christianity. |
| 1081 | Normans enter Albania from Italy and govern until C. 1100. |
| 1096 | Armies of the first Crusade march through Albanian lands. |
| 1190 | Proclamation of the feudal State of Arberia, in the north of Albania, with Kruje as the capital. |
| 1204 | Conquest of Constantinople by the Crusades. Decline of the Empire of Byzantine, Michael Comnenus, member of Byzantine Imperial family founds his despot of Epirus. He |

|  |  |
|---|---|
|  | deprives Byzantine of Albania's coastal region. |
| 1272 | Charles I, King of Naples, enters Albania from northern Italy, forms the kingdom of Arberia and proclaims himself, King of Albania. While the interior of Albania is ruled by Byzantine and Serbian princes till 1356. Roman Catholic religion is spread. |
| 1344 | Albania becomes part of the Kingdom of Serbia, under the leadership of Stephen Dushan together with Macedonia, Thesaly and Epirus. After his death, Albania falls to native chieftains and the Knight Balsha establishes a dynasty at Shkoder, fending off Serbs and Bulgarians. |
| 1352 | Ottoman conquest of Europe begins. |
| 1431 | Turks capture Janina, take a large part of Albania under their control. |
| 1433 | Uprising against the Turks right across the territory from north to south, under the leadership of Arianit Shpata. |
| 1442 | November 28, Gjergj Kastriot Scanderbeg resigns from the Turkish army, enters Kruje with 300 Albanians, proclaims independence of principality of Kastriot and raises his red family flag, with a Black Eagle at the centre, eventually becoming Albania's national flag. |
| 1444 | March, league of Lezhe. The Albanian feudal nobility unite and enter conflict against the Turks under the leadership of Gjergj Scanderbeg. |

| | |
|---|---|
| 1450 | Scanderbeg concludes a peace treaty with Venice to have a free hand in his struggle against the Turks. |
| 1450 | Turkish Sultan Murad, besieges Kruje for five months, but is defeated by Scanderbeg aided by Alfonso I of Naples. |
| 1455 | Scanderberg attacks the Turks at Berat but loses 6,000 men. |
| 1457 | Turks attack Scanderberg with an army of 60,000 and conquer most of the Albanian lowlands and attack his Kruje stronghold, but Scanderberg forces an Ottoman withdrawal. |
| 1463 | Great war between the Turks and Venetians. |
| 1466 | Sultan Muhammad II conquers Albania but fails to occupy Kruje. |
| 1468 | January 17, Scanderberg falls ill with fever and dies in Lezhe. |
| 1478 | Scanderberg's Kruje fortress falls to the Turks. The crucial battle in Albanian history. Muhammad II retrieves Kruje, however Shkoder holds out. |
| 1479 | January 25, peace is concluded with the rest of Albania. Venetians give up Shkoder and the Albanian stations along the coastline., but keep Ulqinj, Antivari and Durres. |
| 1501 | The Ottoman Empire occupies all Albania, with Durres the last town to be taken from the Venetians and Albania remains under Ottoman control until 1912. |

| | |
|---|---|
| 15-16th C. | Thousands of Albanians are forced to emigrate due to hunger and oppression, mainly to southern Italy. |
| 16th C. | The Orthodox church is dominant in the south, the Roman Catholic church in the north. |
| 1555 | Gjon Buzuku publishes the first book in Albanian language 'Meshari' the Messar. |
| 1571 | Turks take Ulqinj from the Venetians. |
| 1614 | Sulejman Pasha Bargjini, builds a mosque, a bath house and a bakery in Tirana. |
| 1635 | Frang Bardhi publishes the first latin - Albanian dictionary and Andre Bogdani writes the first Latin - Albanian Grammar. |
| 1670 | Mehmet Bushati, pasha of Shkoder, rallies his northern chieftains to defeat the Turks. His son Mahmut routes three Turkish armies, but his grandson is defeated in southern Albania. |
| 18th C. | In the late 18th century two Albanian nobles, Ali Pasha Bushatlli and Ali Pasha Tepelena succeeded in establishing semi-independent Pashaliks. Centred respectively at Shkoder in the north and Janina (now in Greece) in the south. Both these autonomous units were suppressed during the first years of the 19th Century. |
| 1878 | A new Albanian league was set up at a congress held in Prizren (now in Yugoslavia) and branches were set up all over Albania. |
| 1912 | In November 1912, Ismail Qemali proclaimed Albanian independence. |

| | |
|---|---|
| 1913 | The European great powers at the London Conference of Ambassadors, drew the boundaries of the new state of Albania, separating from it territory occupied by about half of the Albanian population. |
| 1914 - 1918 | First World War. Albania is overrun by Montenegrin, Austrian, Italian, French, Greek, Bulgarian and Serbian troops. |
| 1915 - 1917 | Albania is occupied and partitioned; Austria - Hungary takes the north; Italy the south west; Greece takes the south and France takes Korce. |
| 1915, | 1st Apr, Greece proclaims full annexation of southern Albania as 'Northern Epirus' |
| 1920 | Congress of Lushnje at which the Albanian constitution is established, a new government is formed. |
| 1921 | 25th Jun, Albania's frontiers are discussed by the Council of League of Nations. |
| 1921 | 9th Nov, Conference of Ambassadors recognises Albania's independence, but also Italy's 'special interests' in Albania. |
| 1921 | 28 Dec, Elections are held to National Assembly and western style political parties emerge. Democratic party, Popular party, Progressive party. Ahmet Zogu becomes Interior Minister. |
| 1922 | 1st Aug, At the Congress of Berat, the Albanian Orthodox church constitutes itself as a church independent of the Patriarch of Constantinople. |

| | |
|---|---|
| 1922 | 2nd Dec, Ahmet Bej Zogolli, leading tribal chief, forms a government; Zogu is both Prime Minister and Interior Minister. |
| 1923 | Popular dissatisfaction with Zogu; Groups rally against him. |
| 1924 | 16th Jan, Liberal-Democratic government of Fan Noli is elected, depriving the Progressive party's Ahmet Zogu of power. He flee's to Yugoslavia. Noli announces agrarian reforms to abolish feudalism and makes certain changes to the constitution, however does not have time to come into effect. |
| 1924 | 19th Feb, Zogu signs a commercial treaty with Italy. |
| 1924 | 1st Sep, Yugoslav troops enter Albania. Fan Noli's government is overthrown by December 23rd and flee's to Vlora. Zogu enters Tirana on December 24th and is restored to power as Prime Minister with a force of Yugoslav mercenaries. |
| 1925 | 15th Jan, Ahmet Zogu assumes supreme power as commander in chief and forms a new cabinet. January 31st, Zogu is elected first President of the Albanian republic. |
| 1925 | 21st Mar, Ramiz Alia is born of a poor muslim family in Shkoder. |
| 1926 | 11th Nov, Zogu signs the Treaty of Tirana 'Pact of Friendship and Security' with Italy. |
| 1928 | 11th Sep, Constituent Assembly proclaims Albania a Kingdom; Zogu is declared Zog I, King of Albanians. |

| | |
|---|---|
| 1938 | Zog marries Geraldine Appony, Hungarian aristocrat, their son Leka is born March 1939. |
| 1939 | 7th April, King Zog and his family flee into exile to Greece then Turkey. Italian occupation. Through the Second World War Zog lives in Buckinghamshire, England, later settling in Cannes and dying in Paris 1961. |
| 1941 | Meeting of the Korce, Shkoder and Youth communist groups in Tirana to establish the communist party of Albania. |
| 1943 | Enver Hoxha is appointed as party secretary. |
| 1944 | 11th Sep, Occupation of Albania by Nazi Germany. May 24th - 28th Enver Hoxha is appointed commander of the armed forces. |
| 1944 | 28th Nov, Liberation of shkoder and thus the liberation of Albania is completed. November 29th is celebrated as the day of Liberation. |
| 1946-47 | Britain and USA break diplomatic relations with Albania. |
| 1948 | 1st Nov, At first Communist party congress the name of the Party is changed to the Party of Labor of Albania. All other party's are banned. |
| 1949-53 | Various British backed attempts to overthrow Hoxha's regime are made, however they are thwarted by Kim Philby's espionage information to the Soviets. |
| 1955 | 14th Dec, Albania enters the U.N.O. unhindered by the UK and USA who abstain rather than use their veto. |

| | |
|---|---|
| 1957 | Albania's first University opens in Tirana, The State University of Tirana, with 3,600 students and 200 staff. Later growing to 17,000 students and 800 staff. In 1991 three further University's were set up in Shkoder, Elbasan and Tirana. |
| 1960 | 3rd Dec, Albania breaks off diplomatic relations with the USSR. Diplomatic relations between China and Albania are strengthened. Between 1953-70, China approves upto $400 in credits. |
| 1967 | Churchs, mosques and other religious institutions are closed. The people are prohibited to pray legally. |
| 1970 | 25th Oct, Electricity officially reaches all Albanian settlements. |
| 1978 | Albania breaks off diplomatic relations with China on mainly ideological grounds. |
| 1981 | 1st Nov, Rejection of China's 'Socialist, Imperialist' policies. |
| 1983 | Signs of a slight softening of relations with China. |
| 1985 | Mar, Meetings are held between Albania and Britain in Paris to settle the Gold/Corfu compensation issues, but nothing is resolved. |
| 1985 | 11th Apr, Death of the party leader, Enver Hoxha, aged 76 of heart failure aggravated by diabetes. April 13th, election of Ramiz Alia as the new President. |
| 1987 | Sept, Diplomatic relations are established with Canada and then West Germany. |

| | |
|---|---|
| 1989 | 1st Aug, Visit to Albania by Mother Terasa, an Albanian national. |
| 1990 | May, Visit to Albania by the United Nations Secretary General Perez de Cueller. |

Congressman Tom Lantos and former Congressman Joseph Dioguardi arrive in Albania for a three day stay with Ramiz Alia.

July, demonstration in Tirana culminates in a number of people rushing into various foreign embassies and requesting asylum. Ferries carrying Albanian emigrants arrive at Brindizi, Italy.

The restoration of diplomatic links with the Soviet Union is announced.

August, Ramiz Alia meets for talks with representatives of the Albanian intellegencia. Unconfirmed reports of major disagreements between Alia and Ismail Kadare.

October, Ismail Kadare announces defection to France.

Balkan conference of Six Foreign Ministers meets in Tirana.

December, Mother Teresa pays her second visit to Albania.

Disturbances at the University Campus in Tirana over living conditions, the police intervene to disperse demonstrators.

The formation of the Democratic Party legalised on December 18th. The Multi Party system is officially allowed and leads to the formation of twelve parties.

1991 February 20, a few thousand demonstrators protesting in the capital, Tirana, topple down the statue of Enver Hoxha.

Religion is legalized, the religious institutions are open and the ex-persecuted priests and hoxhas are allowed to exercise their profession freely.

March 31, elections are organized all over Albania. The Party of Labour (reformed as Socialist Party) wins the elections.

June, the formation of coalition government for national stability.

Dec, Collapse of the coalition government forced by the Democratic party, because the Socialists are seen to be stalling on the reform programme.

1992 March, the Democratic party wins a landslide victory in the General Election with over 65% of the popular vote.

April, Dr Sali Berisha is sworn in as the new President. The new government vows to implement a wide ranging reform programme which will affect all aspects of life in Albania.

# TRAVEL ITINERARY

ALBANIA - "A shore unknown, which all admire,
but many dread to view"

Lord Byron

Guiding tourists has been quite an experience for us. It revealed a new chapter in our lives, a chapter filled with joy and sorrows, laughter and bitterness : laughter caused by the innumerable adventures and sorrows lead by the limited possibilities to expose the truth in an isolated country, as Albania used to be. Regardless of the great limitations faced by the guides, because of the lack of democracy, we did our utmost to make the tourists enjoy themselves in Albania.

On this occasion we would like to thank all the tourists who visited Albania, for their warm appreciation of Albania and for both of us.

Agim Neza & Miranda Hanka

*Travelling through the country.*

Three years ago working as tour guides, we felt embarrassed, because when tourists set foot in Albania, they were asked by the customs officer to fill in a declaration, if they possessed any of the goods, which were a threat to the socialist society, such as : TV set, camera, recorder, transmitter and receiver radio sets, refrigerator, washing machine and other house commodity: watches, drugs, religious books, pornographic magazines, different currencies and if not declared the tourists were considered as smugglers so they were not allowed to visit Albania.

We recall, in March 1990, guiding a group of 17 journalists (who were obliged to hide their profession, as journalists were not allowed to visit the country) and four muslims living in England. The four muslims were very sad because they had their precious kurans confiscated at the customs house of Han i Hoti boarder. So, the guides as always were "a pig in the middle" being obliged to explain the inert rules defined by the Stalinist regime of Albania, the conductor of which was Enver Hoxha, (the first secretary of P.L.A and the leader of Albania). For fifty years in succession Albania was locked in its shell and for this Enverist theory had its argument:

> "Why should we turn our land into an inn with doors flung open to pigs and sows, to boys and girls with pants on at all?
>
> Why should we let the longhaired hippies supplant with their wild orgies the graceful dances of our people"?
>
> E. Hoxha

The students at school, the workers at the factory, even the pedestrians on the street were confronted with big slogans decorating the walls, showing how "cruel" the foreign invasion is, how much the capitalist countries "envy" the victory of socialism in Albania and how "hard" they try to destroy Albania.

The foreigners were considered as spies, recruited by CIA or KGB and as such they were bugged. Therefore Albanians, tried to avoid any suspicious "greeting" or "smiling" with the foreigners, a thing which is not in their friendly and hospitable nature. At one of the Party Congresses it was said; "One of the greatest victories of socialism in Albania, is the creation of the new man" - yes, it was a new breed of humans in Albania, it was the robot - type, instructed by the central system - which was the P.L.A., and if one of the robots disobeyed orders it had to be destroyed, as they were a danger to the others". And the system worked perfectly "the people were happy" - George Orwell would really be fascinated to see his "1984" exercised so faithfully.

With the political changes in the country (1990 - 1993) tourists can now talk freely to the locals and in many cases they are invited to their houses. Similarly, the tourists are allowed to bring everything to Albania with the exception of drugs and weapons. You can now gain your visa at the custom office for USD$40.00.

*Introduction to the Three Itinerary's.*

The following three Itinerary's are based upon years of experience in guiding groups of foreign visitors to Albania. We have written each of the routes with a mixture of detailed historical interest together with some of our own memorable experiences. Thus the text is mixed with some Albanian humour, tourist experiences and folk tales. The combination of towns and villages chosen throughout the three itinerary's have been designed both for the tourist group and individual traveller and will take you to all four corners of this wonderful country.

This way we hope you will develop an understanding of the Albanian culture both past and present and an insight into the friendliness of the Albanian people of today.

# ITINERARY - ONE

ITINERARY - ONE.

SHKODRA - LEZHA - KRUJA - DURRES - KAVAJA - LUSHNJA - FIER - TEPELENA - GJIROKASTRA - SARANDA - KANINA - VLORA - BERAT - TIRANA.

Most tourists in the past have chosen the route through the Yugoslav boarder. The road from Ha i Hoi boarder (Inn of Hoi) to Shkoder passes through the mountain region of Kastrati, from where it proceeds through the small plain that stretches along the shores of Shkodra lake. Another road leads in the direction of "Malesia e Madhe", a rich region with ethnographic peculiarities and picturesque villages, dense forests and green meadows. Passing through the village of Koplik, you can see Shkodra lake which communicates with the sea through Buna river. In ancient times, it was called the lake of Labeates, after the name of the local Illyrian tribe.

From Koplik another road leads towards the mountain health resorts of Rasma, Boga and Thethi. Thethi is a picturesque Alpine village, very much preferred by Albanian's. The road from Koplik to Shkodra is 18 km long, where our journey across Albania begins.

*SHKODRA* : is a town of 71,000 inhabitants. The people of this area are famous for their subtle humour and sense of entertainment. They speak a typical northern dialect of the district, with an accent.

Shkodra was known as an old artisan centre, as well as road and river junction with a considerable transit trade. Shkodra (formerly Scutari) is the third largest town in Albania. It is one of the oldest towns in Europe, having been in the third century B.C. the capital of the Illyrian Kingdom of the Ardians whose queen was the Legendary Teuta.

In 168 B.C the Romans occupied Shkodra and when the Roman Empire split, in 395 A.D, it became part of Byzantine (Eastern) Empire. In 1350, it became the capital of the Albanian Feudal Lords, the Balshas, only to be occupied in 1936 by the Venetians, who held the town for almost 100 years. In 1478 the fortress was besieged by the armies of the turkish Ottoman Empire. In 13th century, it became the capital of the semi-independent pashalik, administrated by the Albanian feudal lords, the Bushatllis.

Shkodra suffered the invasion of the Montenegrins (1913) - with the outbreak of the first World War it suffered the invasion of Serbs, Austrians, Italians and French.

The people of Shkodra gave a great contribution during the second World War, liberating the country from Italian and German invasion. Shkodra was the last town to be liberated on November 28, 1944.

Today Shkodra is an important centre of industry. Its industrial enterprises are: the electric wire and cable works (U.M.B. - 1955) ; the "Drini" plant for spare parts for power stations: the wood and paper working combine: fabric works (1947); a leather and footwear and foodprocessing works.

In Shkodra you will find accommodation at "Rozafa" hotel, situated in the centre of the town. This hotel is among few hotels provided with a lift. There is a restaurant, a souvenir shop (selling Albanian handicraft, cognac, Albanian musical instruments, Albanian folk dress etc) and a bar serving in national currency in the lobby of the hotel. At the reception you may buy Albanian postcards, maps of Albania, stamps, and books in English, French etc. Sometimes, you will find a nice band at the bar of the hotel, playing typical music of the district.

*What to visit;*

One of the most fascinating things to see is "Rozafa" fortress, situated at the top of the hill, south direction, over-looking the town. You can't drive up to the fortress, as it is very steep, so you have to walk about 10 minutes, through the narrow and stony path that snakes to the big iron gate of the fortress.

Entering the front gate you will be astonished by the high milky walls, shaped into arches, and all this reminds you of the legend related to the fortress;

Three brothers were engaged in the building of the original walls of the fortress, but found that everything they constructed, collapsed during the night. An old seer informed them that the successful building of the walls demanded a human sacrifice, and the brothers agreed to sacrifice whichever of their wives brought them their lunch the next day. But the two elder brothers warned their wives, so that the lunch was brought by the wife of the youngest brother. This young woman, Rozafa, agreed to be immured within the walls, provided a hole was left through which she would feed her baby. and still today, milky water flows from a spring within the walls of the fortress, from it is said, the breast of the entombed mother.

This legend walks along with you through all the visit. But it is in the museum of the fortress, where the statue of Rozafa feeding her baby, makes the legend more striking. In this museum you will be acquainted with the history of the fortress. There are objects exhibited which testify to its historical importance. The foundations of the fortress were laid by the Illyrians in the last millennium B.C. Most of its existing walls were constructed during the Middle Ages by the Venetians and Turks. The fortress is oval in shape with 7 towers. three sets of walls divide the fortress into three parts : in the first part there are no buildings; in the second part stand the remains of a mosque, built upon the ruins of a church, together with those of what is believed to have been the barracks; in the third part are the ruins of a palace, which later was turned by the Turks into a munitions dump, the entrance to an underground passage which once linked the fortress with the river Drin and water cisterns, which supplied the occupants with water during the many sieges. At the top of the fortress you will have a clear view of the three rivers, the Buna, Kiri and Drini, which flow into the Adriatic sea.

Descending from the fortress, down to the right, adjacent to the walls of the fortress, stands the Cathedral of St. Stephen, built in the 13th century. After the turkish invasion, the Cathedral was turned into a mosque of which part of the minaret remains.

After the visit you can enjoy fresh drinks, spirits turkish coffee etc, in a characteristic bar, located in the interiors of the fortress. At the same time, inside the museum there is a souvenir shop selling items you may find of interest.

The Leaden Mosque, so called from the lead which covers the one large and 19 smaller cupolas. It is also known as the mosque of Mehmet Pasha Plaku. This mosque was constructed in 1774. Near by is a hamam (Turkish bath of 13th century).

The Catholic Church, built in the late 19th century and at the time the largest in the Balkans, was transformed into a sports centre in 1967 and now it has reverted to its former function. This church is of great importance, because Shkodra was formerly the centre of the Catholic Church in Albania and a

Jesuit seminary was established here in the mid 19th century. During a discussion we had with father Gjergj Simoni and father Zef Simoni, we were informed that the Pope himself has promised to participate on the inauguration of the church in Shkodra.

Mesi Bridge. It is a medieval bridge which spans the Kiri river, 8 km northeast of Shkodra. It is one of the most exquisite bridges ever build by local master builders. The bridge is 112 metres long, made up of three arches, the largest of which is 27 metres long and 15 metres high.

On the way back to Shkodra you will see a free market where peasants sell different goods privately (a thing which was not allowed two year's ago).

The Exhibition of Local Culture. Before leaving Shkodra, it is worth visiting the exhibition of local culture, opened in 1981, where a series of shop - type museums show the finest products of handicrafts : textiles and costumes, woodcarving, metalwork etc. Shkodra at the same time has a rich and original folklore which has been influenced by the social, historical and geographical position of the region. With regard to the historic epic, it can be said that every important event, was commemorated by the Shkodran people through songs. Those songs are related sometimes with ballads. The epic - legendary songs are sung by one or two persons, accompanied by the characteristic instrument called - lahuta which is the most ancient instrument in Albania. It has one string, which is a hair from a horse's tail.

The region of Shkodra has one of the oldest folk costumes called -Xhubleta, which is made of wood and has the form of an umbrella. Xhubleta is worn by women. It is said that before Scanderbeg's death the women used to wear xhubleta with red lines on it (as a decoration), because of the death of Scanderbeg they changed the red lines into black as a sign of mourning. While the men wear trousers made of wool, white with black lines sideways, called - tirqe, and put on a white woollen cap called -qeleshe.

In the town you rarely see women or men wearing folk dress. It is only in the villages that people are dressed in their local folk dress (not all villages). Sometimes, by chance, you may come across peasants walking in the street, wearing their folk dress.

Leaving Shkodra you cross over the Drini river bridge, leaving behind the quarter of Bahcallek (gardens), a name given to the village during medieval times, because of the innumerable gardens that surrounded it. On April 15, 1979 this area was struck by a severe earthquake and the village of Bahcallek was damaged completely. It was rebuilt in 6 months period at the expense of the state.

On the way to Lezha, tourists can see newly planted blocks of vineyards and fruit tree plantations. On the hills that line up along the road there are new plantations of mulberry trees the leaves of which serve to feed the silkworms, for which the area of Shkoder is famous. Leaving the village of Bushati, the road continues along the foot of Kakarriqi mountains, a dry and rocky low mountain range, where bee-keepers bring their bee-hives to feed on sage that grows here and gives to honey a sweet, aromatic flavour. Facing these mountains, stretches the plain of Zadrima (it used to be swampy until 1947) which is famous for cultivating watermelon.

Before entering the town of Lezha and before crossing the Drini river bridge, the road turns right to Shengjin (7 km away from Lezha). There is a regular bus service connecting the town with the seaport of Shengjin. During the summer, Shengjin is crowded with people coming from all over Albania, especially from the north, to spend their summer vacations on the nice sandy beach of Shengjin. In ancient times the port of Shengjin was known under the name of - Nympheon and afterwards - Caesarea. At the time of the civil war between Caesar and Pompey, Mark Anthony, landed here with reinforcements for Ceasar. The name Shengjin means (Shen - Saint and Gjin - John).

*LEZHA* : is one of the oldest towns in Albania, founded in the IV century B.C. under the Illyrian name of Lis (latin - Lisus).

It is mentioned in documents for the first time on 385 B.C. as having been founded by the tyrant of Syracuse, Dionysis. On a hill near the town are the remains of the old Illyrian walls which divide the ancient city into three parts : the acropolis, the upper city and the lower city. "Lis" became the principal commercial centre and port of the Illyrian state of the Ardians. In 1168 B.C., Lis was seized by the romans, and the city played an active role in the civil war between Pompey and Ceasar. In the 9th century, Lis became part of the Byzantine Empire.

Then up to 1398, it was in the hands of the feudal family the Dukagjins, who surrendered it to the Venetians. On March 2, 1444, an important convention of Albanian princes took place; the famous Albanian league was founded, appointing Gjergj Kastriot Scanderbeg, as a supreme commander in the war against Turkish invasion. It was in Lezha on the 17 of January 1468, after 25 years of victorious battles, that our national hero, Scanderbeg died and was buried.

Today Lezha has a population of 10,000 inhabitants. In the field of industry, Lezha has the most important paper factory in the country, factories for producing sunflower oil, bricks and tiles, prefabricated building and agricultural machinery, fish canning factory, flour mill etc.

*What to visit;*

Scanderbeg's tomb is situated in the interior of St. Nicholas Cathedral (in Albanian - Shenkoll). After the contemporary historian, Martin Barleti, Scanderbeg was buried solemnly in this cathedral on January 1468. In front of the ruins of the cathedral is the bust of the hero with the national flag standing behind it. On Scanderbeg's grave is his sword and the helmet (the originals being in the Art History Museum of Vienna). There are 25 emblems hanging on the walls of the cathedral representing the battles waged, by Scanderbeg and their respective dates.

The cathedral of St. Nicholas was discovered by chance in 1979, during the earthquake. When the Turks occupied the town in 1578, they violated the tomb, shared out his bones to make amulets and turned the cathedral into a mosque. Still on the right wing of the wall has remained a piece of mural from the cathedral of St. Nicholas. Here you may buy postcards and booklets on the history of Lezha.

The Ethnographic Museum, is opened in the characteristic dwelling house of the town. In each room are exhibited objects, folk dresses, photos which give you a clear picture of the district. Here you are acquainted with the traditions of the town and the villages. Wooden furniture, woollen carpets, copper utensils used by the house wives and a model of a shepherd cottage, give a true to life view of the rural life.

In this museum there is a pavilion giving information about the earthquake of 1979 and the huge work done to reconstruct the area.

Besides these interesting places Lezha offers one of the most attractive sights : "The Hunting Lodge" - known as the isle of

Lezha - situated in a beautiful surroundings, 2 km away from the town. "The Hunting Lodge " was the property of Count Ciano, Italian Foreign Minister and Mussolini's son-in-law. Now it functions as a hotel and restaurant. Before lunch, you may take a walk in the surroundings. The willow trees, the fresh air and the small river flowing by, is a relaxation.

"The Hunting Lodge" is quite comfortable inside. The timbered ceiling and carefully planned rusticity of the decor, the open fireplace for winter wood burning and the leather chairs make you feel at home. There are two rooms, still well preserved, where Count Ciano used to sleep. Not far from this place is a sandy island of Kune, rich in pheasant and ducks. thus, at lunch sometimes you are offered the delicious meat of pheasant, duck or fish.

Departing from Lezha, in the direction of Tirana, the visitor travels through the fields of various villages; the road begins at once to ascend and after leaving the mountains of Pedhane, you reach the banks of Mati river, with its widespread banks. At Mati bridge you leave the road that leads to the region of Mirdita (Good Day). After crossing Mati bridge, you enter Miloti, a road junction and a small centre of an agricultural region. On the right, there is the Chemical Superphosphate Plant of Lac. the road here, is at all hours crowded with traffic. The huge majority of vehicles are tough Chinese and Russian trucks, built to cope with difficult roads. The traffic is worse now, that the state has allowed the people to have private cars. If "Mercedes Benz" some months ago was a luxurious car, belonging only to the members of the Polit Bureau, now it is common, used by the people who can afford to buy it, or those supported by their relatives living abroad. You can tell a private car from a government one by the signs on their number plates.

The traffic in Albania is not well organised. Different from other countries here : "the people are not afraid of cars, on the contrary, the drivers are scared to death, seeing hundreds of pedestrians walking carelessly on the street, so the blowing of the horns sometimes is really irritating.

On the other side having minimal means of transportation, many people go hitch-hiking on the road, and drivers (mainly private) give them a lift.

Rarely, you will be confronted by animals (esp. driving through the rural area ) which sometimes cause a traffic jam. Besides lorries, and other vehicles, "efficient" means of transportation are ox-carts and horse-carts (the latter used in the capital as well, for Public Services). These are rare things for the visitors, who never miss the chance to take pictures of them. These means of transportation are temporary, as in the future, with the development of the economy and improvement of the roads, ox-carts and horse-carts will exist no more.

Leaving the town of Lac and passing Fushe - Kruja (Kruja on the plain) you take the road to Kruja. To the south of the road, on a hillside near the village of Zgerdhesh, are the ruins of the ancient city of "Albanopolis", the capital of the Illyrian tribe of Albanoi, which flourished from the end of third century A.D. It's name is mentioned for the first time by Ptolemy, in the second century A.D. In the forth century, its inhabitants abandoned the city and moved up the hill to the more defendable position of Kruja. It is from the Illyrian tribe, that the country started to be called "Albania" and the people "Albanians". In the seventeenth the century we, Albanians, called our language "Shqipe" and the country "Shqiperia" Albanian scholars believe that this name is derived not from "Shqipe" (eagle), but from "Shqiptoj" (to speak intelligible).

The road to Kruja is a mountainous one, with olive groves, quarries, lime kilns and cement factory, ending up on the slope of Kruja mountain where the town is situated.

*KRUJA;* has been inhabited since the third century B.C. it is mentioned in records for the first time in the 9th century. By the end of the twelfth century, Kruja had become the capital of the first Albanian principality of Arberia, known for its trade and handicrafts. In the fourteenth century, it became the capital of the principality of the Albanian feudal lords, the Topias. The name of Kruja is related with the name of Gjergj Kastriot Scanderbeg, who fought heroically against the Ottoman invasion.

The youngest of Gjon Kastrioti's four sons Gjergj, was sent with his three brothers as hostage to the Sultan at Constantinople in 1415. He became famous at the military school and he was given the Islamic name "Iskander" (Albanian - Skender) and the title "beg" for valour on the battle field. In 1443, he suddenly left the Ottoman army fighting Hunyadi, the Hungarian hero, and returned to Albania, where on November 28, 1443, with an army of 300 horsemen raised the Albanian flag in front of the people of Kruja.

The Turkish armies besieged the fortress of Kruja four times, in, 1450, 1466, 1467, but they were driven off. In 1478 (ten years after the death of Scanderbeg), after the Turkish victory, the turks failed to change the name of the fortress of Kruja to Akcehisan.

During 15th century, Scanderbeg played a great role for the liberation of the country. Scanderbeg fought 25 battles (one battle in a year) and lost only two.

*What to Visit;*

The fortress; This was built in the 5 & 6th centuries A.D., after the abandonment of Albanopolis. the walls were rebuilt in 13th century by Charles I of Anjou and again some centuries later by the Turks. In 1617 an earthquake caused great damage to the walls. The walls are reinforced with 11 (eleven) towers. Thereafter it passed to the Thopia family, who strengthened it still further. The Turks captured the place in 1396; were driven out soon afterwards but returned in 1415.

At the entrance, behind the gate, have remained some small niches, apparently designed for the guards and small square.

The administration and military buildings used to be located way up, where a few houses stood. This is the highest and at the same time the best defended part of the fortress. A tower, transformed later into a clock tower (known as the eyrie) stands. From this part of the Fortress, one obtains a magnificent view. Looking down at the abyss, one can see very clearly the natural defences of the fortress.

Near the tower stands the mosque (formerly a Christian Church) while the remains have also been excavated of a Christian Church with mural paintings.

To the west of the fortress lies a 15th century hamam (Turkish bath) and the former Bektashi monastery, the Dollma Teqe, constructed in 1789. the Bektashi were a mystical Muslim sect founded in Anatolia in the 13th century by Haxhi Bektash Veli. Bektashism did not insist on the veiling of women or abstention from alcohol. It preached non violence and the brotherhood of men. When the Turkish government suppressed Bektashism in 1925, the headquarters of the sect were transferred to Albania and the Albanian Kryegjysh (Chief Grandfather) became World Grandfather to all Bektashis - estimated before 1939 at 7 million.

Another interesting building is the reconstructed medieval town hall, near to the Eyrie. To the left of the main entrance is erected the Museum of Gjergj Kastriot Scanderbeg, opened in 1982. The building is designed as an ancient fortress; such a thing gives to it a special interest. the museum is composed of separate pavilions reflecting the life and activity of Scanderbeg. Each pavilion completes a part of the heroic struggle against Ottoman invasion. Here you find the echo of the 25-years long war, in innumerable historical and literary works, portraits and sketches. In the third pavilion, there is one of the biggest modern murals in Albania, 182 square metres, painted by an Albanian amateur who lives in Tirana. the mural shows the strategy used by Scanderbeg in defeating the Turkish armies. In front of the mural lie the helmet and the sword of Scanderbeg (the originals are displayed in the museum of Vienna).

Something which arouses the interest of tourists is the symbol of the goat's head on Scanderbeg's helmet.

The goat's head on Scanderbeg's helmet remained since the second battle, when Scanderbeg and his army were besieged by the Turks in the castle. As there was no other way out, Scanderbeg played a trick to the enemies; at night, he let a flock of goats with candles on their horns, through a secret passage. The Turks deceived by the lights of the candles on goats horns followed the flock through the passage. Taking advantage of the enemies confusion, Scanderbeg attacked them successfully. Since that time Scanderbeg decided to keep a goat's head on his helmet to commemorate his victory.

Having been introduced to Scanderbeg's life and the struggle against Turkish invasion, you may take pictures of the town and the costal plain below, from the terrace on the third floor. This museum offers postcards and brochures with illustrations on the material exhibited and from the town of Kruja.

After visiting this museum, you may have coffee at a characteristic two-storied house which is a stone throw from the museum. the wooden chairs and tables, the fire-place, give the oriental atmosphere to the coffee-house. Sometimes groups have meals in the restaurant on the ground floor. they are usually served a spicy local meal called - "fergese" - (made of sour milk, eggs, pieces of liver and red pepper); this dish is served hot, and it normally accompanied by a characteristic spirit, called "raki" (made of grapes). After the meal, you may have turkish coffee, in characteristic cups, which is stronger than expresso.

The Bazaar: One of the most interesting features is the old Bazaar consisting of rows of shops, workshops with wide eaves, to protect the customers from the weather. The Bazaar was reconstructed in 1965 - 1967 as it used to be in the 18th century. The visitor may buy souvenirs at some local shops, where all kinds of handicraft objects are exhibited. You may buy souvenirs with national currency or foreign currency. The most sought after is "Scanderbeg" cognac, which has a high quality taste.

Leaving Kruja behind, on the right an automobile road enters a narrow valley, where a route has been blasted along a hard rocky mountain slope, comes out into a rich pine-tree forest and leads to Qafe Shtame. Qafe Shtame is a mountain resort. The dense forests, the ice cold water, the pure air and the beautiful places of excursion, have made it a much frequented centre.

On the way to Vora (a small living centre), a road poster indicates the direction to Rinas airport, the only commercial airport in the country.

From the village of Vora, the road to Durres continues westwards. The fields on both sides of the road are planted with industrial plants like, cotton, sunflower, vineyards, cherry-trees etc.

Another thing that strikes your eyes is the large number of concrete - mushrooms, bunkers.

These military objects are a puzzle to all the tourists travelling through Albania. They have caused prolonged discussions among visitors.

- Why do you have so many bunkers?
- What time were they built?
- What do you need them for now? .... etc.

To these innumerable questions there are innumerable answers; some are convincing, some other are far from being convincing. We will give you many reasons and you, dear readers, may judge for yourselves :

1) Bunkers were built, because Albania, historically, has been at the gun point by other countries. Europe has been cruel to Albania (recall 1913, the division of the territory).

2) Bunkers were built after the liberation (1944) (especially in the 60's when the relations between Russia and Albania broke off).

3) The increasing number of bunkers corresponds with the ever increasing number of homeless (...... $ per bunker) and a very stingy policy regarding apartments; 2 - 3 couples living in a two-roomed apartment.

4) Bunkers played a double role : to defend the country from "a possible invasion" and to remind Albanian's of the strong dictatorship, making them "loyal" to the system and the Party of Labour.

5) Bunkers were part of a 45-years long experiment made by some Albanian marxist - leninist scientists, to prove what a single country can do on its own, in contrast with the rest of the world. The experiment had positive results; Albania is unique in its type, there is no capitalist or socialist country to mat it. Can you find any other country in Europe with so many bunkers?

But the "gordon knot" is the role of these bunkers in the future, which sometimes is solved by "bunker photo - stop".

An American referred to the bunkers as a profitable means for Albania, if sold to the Hollywood Film Studio, for producing war-films.

Another suggestion was that the bunkers could be used as bars for selling coca-cola and other drinks.

Leaving behind the bunker puzzle, you cross the Erzeni river bridge and finally enter the bathing beach area of Durres. Here are some rest and recreation homes for schoolchildren and working people. A beautiful bathing beach with the finest of sands and an equally wonderful sea, welcome the tourists.

In the centre of the beach are situated tourist - hotels : "Adriatic", "Durres", "Apollonia", "Adriatic" hotel is one of the best in Albania. Situated on the beach, opposite the sea, with its wide veranda on the back side, makes it very much preferred by the visitors. The hotel has a restaurant on the ground floor and a bar serving in hard currency, opposite it. At the entrance of the hotel, on the left is a book shop and further on, a souvenir shop. There is also a taverna which opens at 11 p.m. There, you are offered several drinks and a small band entertains the visitors with Albanian and foreign music.

These hotels are crowded in the summer, when the tourists come to spend their vacations on the beach of the Adriatic sea. Quite often with organised excursions to other towns near by.

*It is unusual in Albania to go naked on the beach. it happened once, guiding a group, that two women went topless. Such a thing caused confusion to the locals and irritated the hotel - authorities, who asked the guides to explain the situation to the Hungarians. The two ladies were surprised "What's the fuss about us going topless? Don't the hotel authorities have other business to do? We thought Albanian's would like our beautiful bodies!"*

Dear readers, nudism in Albania is not allowed by law. There is a special article on the penal system that punishes nudism on the beach or other public places. On the other side, it has to do with the customs, traditions and of course mentality of the people. It has to do with what one may consider as moral or immoral, as right or wrong.

After spending a night on the beach, you may drive to Durres, which is only 5 km away.

<u>DURRES</u> : formerly Durrazzo, is one of the oldest towns in Albania. The legend says that it was founded by Epidamnos, the Illyrian King of the area, who called it by his own name and named the port area after his grandson - Dyrrah. In 1627 - 1626 B.C. Greeks from Corfu and Cornith invaded the area and called the town Dyrrachion. In the 4th century B.C. Dyrrachion had become an independent city - state, producing metalwork, pottery, fabrics, leather and ships and its coins

were circulating throughout the ancient world. The Illyrians after establishing their own state, tried to place Durres under their own dependence. In this struggle, victory favoured the state of the Taulantes.

The Illyrian king Monunes, minted coins in Durres, with his own name in them and made Durres, the centre of his own state. In 229 B.C. Durres was taken by rome and under roman rule, the town was called Dyrrachium, which became the starting point of the "Via Egnatia", linking roam with the East. The famous Roman orator, Cicero called durres "an admirable city ...", while the poet Catullus called it "the tavern of the Adriatic".

After the partition of the Roman Empire, Durres remained part of the Eastern Empire, Byzantium.

During the 10th & 14th centuries, the town was captured by Bulgarians, Normans, Crusaders, Venetians, Angevins and

Serbs. In 1501 it was invaded by the Turks. In 1914 - 1920 Durres became the capital of Albania. In 1915 it became the seat of Prince Velhelm Xuvid. In 1916 was temporarily occupied by Serbian forces. On the 7th of April 1939, Durres was occupied by Italians.

Today Durres is one of the biggest towns and sea ports in Albania. It has a population of 82,000 inhabitants. Durres has a chemical enterprise, agricultural machinery works, cigarette factory, radio and television works etc.

*What to visit;*

The Fortress of the City : the remains of the walls belong to the 6th century; the addition from 13-14th century. Ana Comnena, the daughter of the Byzantine Emperor, Alexis Comnenius, describing the fortress, writes that "its walls were so thick that 4 horsemen could ride abreast on top of them". Wars and earthquakes destroyed the fortress.

The Amphitheatre : It is one of the biggest and most exquisite monuments that have survived from the ancient city. It was built in the 2nd century A.D. In the early Middle Ages, it was abandoned. In the 10th century, a chapel and cemetery were built upon its areas and galleries.

From the records of the amphitheatre must have been very big, with a capacity of 15,000 spectators. Its diameter must have been more than 120 metres. The amphitheatre was unearthed by chance in 1966, by a citizen digging in his garden. Because of the successful earthquakes that shook the city, only 1/3 of ancient Dyrrachium has been excavated. The archaeologists are facing enormous problems, as they need to destroy most of the houses built upon the ancient ruins (such a thing needs large investments and a lot of time).

The Belle of Durres : It is the most polychromatic mosaic found in the country. The mosaic was discovered beneath a dwelling, in a residential quarter of the town. It is elliptical in shape and measures 17 x 10 feet. The mosaic depicts on a block ground g woman's head surrounded by flowers. You may see it in the museum of National History in Tirana.

Roman Thermal Baths : were discovered on 1962, during the construction of the Palace of Culture. The baths have a "hypocaust" or heating system and a pool, 23 feet long by 17 feet wide.

The Archaeological Museum : situated near the sea, is rich in objects excavated in durres. It gives a view on the ancient Dyrrachium. There are many objects excavated in Durres and this museum being small can not reveal all of them, so it is decided to build another museum (a larger one) next to the existing.

Durres underground has been declared a "cultural monument" and no new construction is permitted here without the approval of the Institute of Cultural Monuments.

On the west side of the town, on top of a hill, rises a magnificent villa. It used to be the villa of King Zog. Today it is used to receive foreign delegations. The villa overlooks the port of Durres and its semi-circle balcony gives a complete view to the scenery.

The last thing to be seen at the entrance of Durres, is the train station.

Next town to be visited is Fier. The road to Fier passes through sandy beaches. Here along automobile road rises steep huge rock, the rock of Kavaja. It is the ancient Petra where Caesar and Pompey established the camps of their respective armies, in the year 54 B.C., during the Civil War. At the end of the 11th century, a big battle took place between the Normans, who had besieged Durres and the Emperor Alexis Comnenus; the battle ended with the victory for the Normans.

*KAVAJA* : is mentioned for the first time in the 15th century under the name of Kavalje. In the late Middle Ages it became an important trading centre, especially in grain and a craft centre noted for its pottery and dairy produce. In the town centre is the mosque (which now is functioning).

Today Kavaja has a population of 23,000 inhabitants. It has a glass factory, nail and bolt works, a paper factory and a carpet factory.

Kavaja is the birthplace of Alexander Moisi, the famous actor, who played successfully in the Vienna National Theatre and became known for playing Shakespearean characters.

At Kavaja, parallel with the highway runs the railway and both of them converge at Rrogozhina. The first railway, Durres - Pe - quin - Kavaje, was built in 1947. Since that time, railway transport, has continually increased. In 1983 railway transport accounted for more than 46% of the volume of goods transport. The most important regions of the country are covered with the railway network; Tirana - Durres - Fier - Vlora; Tirana - Elbasan - Pogradec; Tirana - Shkoder - Hani i Hotit: The last one links Albania with the international railway system. A new railway is under construction of Tirana to Burrel.

Rrogozhina : is an important road and railroad junction, where the two branches of the ancient "Via Egnatia" converged - the one that came from Dyrrachium (Durres) and the other from Apollonia, Fier. Rrogozhina has an oil and soap works and a cotton ginning factory.

From Rrogozhina crossing the Shkumbini river bridge, you enter the plain of Myzeque, which is 72 km long. Before the liberation this plain was swampy and boggy, but now it is the main plain for the production of industrial plants and cereals.

In 1948 following the "socialist revolution" in the countryside, the Party of Labour (the only political leadership in the country), collectivised the land. The process of collectivisation was accomplished within a short period of time, thanks to the enormous propaganda exercised by the system in power. The rich peasants and those that were against the collectivisation, were considered as "kulaks" and to be a "kulak" meant to be cursed for the life time. "Waging the class struggle in the countryside means : the political isolation, the economic isolation and elimination of the kulaks as a stratum" - (E.

Hoxha). A kulak was equal to a political prisoner in the sense of human rights. The nieces and nephews of the kulak family, did not have the right to attend studies at the University; no matter how bright they were, they were improper for our socialist society. Sometimes these "kulak predecessors" found themselves in a crossroad; whom to blame - the government? - their grandparents? - or, perhaps, themselves?

The collective farms established on the plain had a high productivity, while those in the mountainous areas, unfavoured by the cold climate and improper terrain conditions for the usage of modern machinery, remained backwards. The main financial resource for the letter was the livestock. Consequently, the collectivization of the livestock in 1967, marked the final economic destruction of the mountainous villages.

With democratic changes in the country, (1991) private property is allowed in the towns and villages. The peasants were given private land and may keep livestock.

Along the seashore of the plain of Myzeque, is to be found one of the most attractive sites, Divjaka. It has bathing beaches and high pine trees rising in its background.

*LUSHNJA* : The small town of Lushnja is mentioned in the 15th century under the name of Lusnie.

In 1920 in Lushnja was held the Congress that demanded the re-establishment of an independent Albanian state. This Congress appointed the new government and proclaimed tirana the capital of Albania. Today Lushnja has a population of 30,000 inhabitants.

Lushnja has factories for the production of plastics, paper building materials, plants for the processing of milk, maize, vegetables and the production of alcoholic drinks.

Driving out of Lushnja (Fier direction), you will notice on the top of a picturesque hill covered with cyprus trees, the 13th century monastery of Ardenica. It had in the past a famous school.

The church was of basilica type; its mural paintings were made by the talented painters, Konstantin and Athanas Shpataraku from the town of Korca. Among the mural paintings you can distinguish the figure of the famous musicologue of the 12th century, Jan Kukuzel from Durres. Among the old icons, a special attention deserves that of Konstantin Shpataraku, a painter iconography of the 18th century, portraying the Albanian prince, Karl Topia.

The monastery is reconstructed and in the interiors are open, a bar, a taverna, a restaurant and some bed rooms, which function regularly for the visitors. The monastery still preserves the traditional style of furniture, such as, wooden divans covered by ship's skin, law wooden stools and tables, decorated rosettes etc. Ardenica is very much preferred by the tourists and locals. Descending Ardenica and winding the way at the foot of the hills, the road crosses the Seman river and from there leads straight to Fier.

*FIER* : was founded in the eighteenth century. It has a population of 37,000 inhabitants. Fier has a cotton gin, brick and tile factory, chemical fertilizer plant, a thermo-electric power station (75,000KW), and oil refinery.

12 km away from Fier, is situated Apollonia, the most important archaeological centre in the country.

Apollonia : was founded at the beginning of the sixth century B.C. (year 588) by the Greek colonists coming from Corinth and Corcyra. Apollonia is one of 30 ancient towns dedicated to the God Apollo. Cicero, described it as "magna urbs et gravis ..." A great and important city". It is situated near Aos river (today Vjosa) and on one of the fertile plains of southern Illyria, inhabited by the Taulantian Illyrians. An important factor, responsible for the economic and cultural development of Illyrian Apollonia, was the exploitation of the riches of the place and the intercourse with the Illyrians.

This made it possible for the town to break away from the mother cities that had founded it.

In the middle of the fifth century B.C. a workshop for minting coins was set up here. Through trade and commercial transactions these coins spread throughout Illyria and beyond its boundaries. Apollonia was conscious of the strength of the Illyrians not only in its surroundings, as it witnessed the establishment of the State of the Taulants, but within the town itself where a great number of Illyrians had settled, occupying some of the highest posts in its administration, economic and cultural life.

By the second century B.C. Apollonia has a population of 55,000 inhabitants. In the first century B.C. Julius Caesar used its citadel as a stronghold against Pompey and as a reward for its support of Caesar, Apollonia was granted the status of a free city. It was a cultural centre, where art, architecture and sculpture flourished. At this time Octavianus Augustus (the first Roman Emperor) and Agrippa, his close friend and associate came to study at the famous school of Apollonia. It was here that they learned the news about the assassination of Caesar.

In the third century A.D. the earthquakes changed the direction of the Aos river and brought the decline of Apollonia.

The Excavations and the Monuments of Apollonia : The first attempts to conduct excavations in Apollonia were made during the first World War, by Austrian archaeologists who unearthed and explored mainly the walls that encircled the city. Systematic excavations began in 1924 by a French archaeological mission headed by Leon Rey, who brought to light a complex of monuments at the centre of the city. A lot of excavations have been made by Albanian archaeologists during the last 20 years. Many objects are exhibited in the museum which has been the monastery of St. Mary.

The Encircling Wall: Apollonia is surrounded by a protecting wall, with a perimeter of some 4,500 metres and a thickness of 3.40 metres. The wall was constructed during the forth century B.C.

The Terraced Wall with the Arched Gates : In the centre of the city a terrace wall has come to light, which is linked with the encircling wall. In front of the wall rises a cylindrical alter, where the people offered their sacrifices before entering the precincts of the temple. Near the altar stands an obelisk dedicated to Apollo.

The Monument of Agonothetes : This monument decorated the centre of the city. The structure had the form of a semicircle and served as an assembly place of the council of the city - the Bule. The front part of the structure was decorated in a special manner: there are 6 pillars crowned with capitals of the Corinthian style. An inscription dating from the middle of the second century A.D. tells that the building was constructed by high ranking officers of the city, a monument with the purpose of commemorating the death of his soldier brother. On the day of the inauguration of the monument, a show was staged in the city with the participation of 25 couples of gladiators.

On the western side, from the top of the monumental structure, the tourists can see the ruins of the small temple of Artemis (Diana). At the eastern side there is a street which passes under a triumphal arch. On the opposite side of the monument of the Agonothetes, there is a colonnade decorated with marble statues.

The Library and the Odeon : rise behind the colonnade. Opposite the monument of Aganothetes stands an Odeon or "a small theatre" for 200 spectators. The building had a stage, an orchestra and tiers. There they gave musical shows, recitals, and held oratorical and philosophical discussions.

The Portico : This portico belonged to the forth & third centuries B.C.; but later on, during the first century, it was reconstructed. the portico was 77 metres long.

The House with Mosaics : A couple of metres away was excavated a rich Apollonian dwelling house of the third century A.D.: The mosaics are of all types. There are mosaics where the main decorative motives are simple geometric figures, others have ornamental mythological figures like : hypocamposes (seahorses), accompanied by Nereids and Erotes. One of the mosaics represents a scene where Archiles holds the wounded Penthesilea, the beautiful queen of Amazones, in his arms. Fontana : represents in itself a complex structure; it had a wall which collected the waters that sprang from the earth, and four other aquaducts.

The Museum of Apollonia : has 7 pavilions, a gallery and 2 porticos. Here are exhibited different objects that testify to the history of Apollonia.

The Church of St. Mary : is situated between the museum and the refectory. The church is of Byzantine style. The interiors of the church had once been painted, but today very few fragments from the mural paintings have remained. The church was built in the fourteenth century. The wall painting represents Emperor Andronicus Paleologus as the builder of the church. The refectory of the monastery was built at the same time as the church.

In our guiding experience we have come across people with different interests and behaviours which vary from touristic to journalistic.

*Three year's ago for instance, were guided a group which seemed to have a "special interest" in the country, but hardly any archaeological. We arrived to Fier at lunch time and decided to*

*make the visit to Apollonia first. We had hardly left Fier, when the British tour guide requested to stay in the hotel as she felt sick. Her suggestion aroused the interest of 4 other tourists who offered to give "first aid" to the sick. The bus stopped and to our surprise all the people (except for 5 tourists - 4 muslims and 1 reporter) jumped out of it. There was a barrage of requests, everyone had an excuse : toilet, interview with the pedestrians, coffee, tooth ache, a town exploration, and the most "convincing" argument was : arranging lunch for the remaining Apollonia visitors. (Two Albanian guides, four muslims and one reporter). You can imagine yourselves the visit to Apollonia. It was funny. The curator, at Apollonia, seeing the five tourists coming out of the bus, asked in surprise : "A fifty-seat bus driving only five tourists?!! It is unusual."*

*But, the biggest surprise came later, when the four muslims facing the sunset, kneeled down on their persian carpets praying to "Allah" and the reporter who had been looking forward to finding proof that Albania is not quite atheist, started to take pictures of them.*

*Those 4 muslims were the first to break the ice and pray in public places in Albania, that was the first sign of the future changes, that we were observing with delight.*

*We arrived back to Fier to find the rest of the group made of, a theatrical agent, a tutor, a hotelier, four teachers, a builder, a horse riding instructor, a bored house wife, an archaeology student, a gallery director, a farmer, a salesman and a British Rail technician, wandering around to get stories for the foreign press and media : "The Observer", "The Independent", "Daily Mail", "Yorkshire Post", "B.B.C." "Sky TV" "RTE" etc.*

*- "It is a very interesting group - stated the British tour guide, Sally (who has been many times in Albania and is very fond of it).*

*- have you noticed that they are fond of taking pictures of your beautiful country?"*

*- "Yes - we answered - we noticed it in Apollonia!"*
*Worried by our ironic answer, she made another attempt to convince us that the group was made of amateur photographers.*

*-"Let's have a photo - stop here- she said enthusiastically to the guides, driving through Muzina pass, - the group will be very pleased to take pictures of this beautiful scenery!" The bus stopped and the guide addressed to the group :*

*- "Well ladies and gentlemen, it is said there are a lot of keen amateur photographers in the group. Here is a nice spot, do you want to get out?"*

*Everybody was making faces and didn't move at all. The guides smiled to the British guide, the British guide tried to smile to the group, but she could produce nothing but a sneer. Willing to accomplish the desire of the tour guide, the group got out of the bus.*

*- The truth, as explained by (journalist at "The Observer" and theatrical agent in Albania) in one of his articles entitled "Albanian Infiltrators" is that - nobody moved because there were no labour camps, no prisons, no foully polluted streams, trickling toxic sludge from a near by factory. No sign, no poster, no monument chiselled into the landscape of the hectoring boarish presence of Enver Hoxha.... in fact there was nothing to photograph at all."*

*We will never forget this group, because it was the first and the last who came to Albania as tourists and left as journalists.*

*Allow us, dear readers to express our great appreciation for the huge work done by the British press and mass media, to expose the reality in Albania.*

The highway from Fier towards Tepelena runs through the oil town of Patos (the seat of the petroleum engineering works), to enter the region of Mallakastra. It proceeds through the small town of Ballsh (the seat of the deep oil refinery) and passes the villages of Hekal and Klos, the sites respectively of the ancient Illyrian cities of Bylis and Nikaia. Crossing through Vjosa river, the road leads to the mining town of Memaliaj. The subsoil of Memaliaj is very rich in coal.

There is a wide range of metallic and non-metallic minerals in Albania. Among them, the principal ones are the reserves of oil, natural gas, bitumen, lignite, iron - nickel, chromium and copper. In chromium mining, Albania ranks third in the world. Leaving Memaliaj you enter the town of Tepelena.

_TEPELENA_ : is situated on a rocky mountain, where the valley of the river Drino joins that of the Vjosa. Here are the remains of a bridge which dates from the second century. Above the bridge a fortress was erected here in the forth & fifth centuries and restored in the tenth & eleventh centuries. In 1789 Tepelena was captured by Ali Pasha Tepelena (1740 - 1822), a powerful Albanian lord, who had set up an autonomous pashalik at Janina (now in Greece).

On Al Pasha's orders a new fortress was constructed in 1819, on the ruins of the medieval fortress. Ali Pasha tried to establish a pashalik, independent from the Turkish empire, but he couldn't succeed. He and his three sons were killed by the Turks. Tepelena and its historical character, Ali Pasha, were a great inspiration to the famous poet George Byron. Lord Byron came to Albania in the Autumn of 1809 and wrote about the contemporary Albanian life in his well know poem : "Childe Harold's Pilgrimage". The poet was invited to the house of Ali Pasha Tepelena about which he writes :

"The vizier received me in a large room paved with marble; a fountain was playing in the centre; the apartment was surrounded by scarlet Ottomans;" and he refers to Ali Pasha:

"....sixty years old, very fat and not tall but with a fine face, light blue eyes and a white beard; his manner is very kind and at the same time he possesses that dignity which I find universal among the Turks"

Lord Byron was struck by the virtues of the Albanian's who are : "brave, rigidly honest and faithful... they are, perhaps the most beautiful race in point of countenance in the world..."

The thing which impressed him mostly, was the hospitality, referring to Ali Pasha, he writes :

"He received me standing, a wonderful compliment from a Muslim and made me sit down in his right hand."

Lord Byron met Albanian's of different strata of the population, regardless of their economic situation, they were very hospitable. The poet gives his impressions in his correspondence. Once he offered to pay an Albanian for his faithfulness and hospitality, but he was refused:

"No - said the Albanian - I want you to be thankful to me and not to pay me!"

Later Byron writes : "I never lost anything and they always invited me to their houses."

Byron makes a vivid description of the nature travelling Tepelena:

"The sun had sunk behind vast Tomerit,
and Laos wide and fierce came roaring by,
the shades of wonted night were gathering yet,
when down the steep banks winding warily,
Childe Harold saw like meteors in the sky,
the glittering minarets of Tepalen,

whose walls or 'erlook the stream;
and drawing nigh, he heard the busy hum of warrior-men
Smelling the breeze that sigh'd along the
lengthening glen."

Besides George Byron, there were a large number of travelling authors in the nineteenth century that wrote about Albania. At that time there were about 150 books published in the U.K. about Albanian origin, history, folklore, traditions (hospitality).

Among the outstanding personalities, who travelled through Albania at that time were : Henry Holland with his book :"Traversing the Jonian Islands Albania; during the Years 1812 and 1813 the well known painter Charles Robert Koksell. Edward Lear (1812 - 1888) "Journal of a Landscape painter in Albania and Illyria" (1851). Edith Durham "High Albania".

About 15 minutes drive from Tepelena, is a nice tourist spot, called "Uji i Ftohte" (cold water). You may have a coffee or other drinks in the bar and enjoy the beautiful scenery. The river Drino flowing by, make this spot more attractive.

After a short relaxation at the "Uji i Ftohte", the road meanders to the museum town of Gjirokastra.

<u>GJIROKASTRA</u> : is one of the most attractive towns in Albania. Gjirokastra (or so called "the town of a thousand stairs"), is of particular interest for its native architecture; the area on which it is built and its form resembling an extended cyclopic hand. The characteristic houses clustered around the majestic fortress towering above them as a huge battle ship, are small fortresses in themselves. The great period of house construction extends from about 1800-1860.

Gjirokastra lies on the slopes of Gjere mountain, overlooking the river Drino. The first traces are to be found in the 1st century A.D; it became an urban centre by the thirteenth century. Gjirokastra is mentioned for the first time in a document of 1336, under the name of Argyropolihne (the township of Argyro), derived, according to the legend from a princess, Argyro, who hurled herself to her death from a tower to avoid falling into the hands of the invaders.

There is another hypothesis, that the name of the town has derived from the Illyrian tribe of Argyres, who are known to have lived in this area.

Later, the town became known as Argyrokastro. Gjirokastra had been under the Byzantine dominion till late fourteenth century, when it passed under the control of the Albanian feudal prince Zanebisha. In the year 1432, Gjirokastra was captured by the Ottoman Turks. At this time Gjirokastra became the seat of the local Albanian feudal lords. In 1811, Ali Pasha Tepelena, after bombarding the fortress with artillery, forced the town to capitulate. Later on, Gjirokastra, was to play an important role as the cradle of the patriotic movement of the Albanian's for freedom and independence. In 1908, the Albanian detachment led by Ceciz Topulli, inflicted heavy casualties on the Ottoman troops. In 1940 - 1941, during the Greek - Italian war, Gjirokastra became, once more a battlefield.

Today, Gjirokastra has a leather factory and a factory for the processing and the fermentation of tobacco, as well as a for manufacturing cigarettes etc.

*What to Visit;*

The Fortress, dates back to the forth & fifth centuries. Situated on a hill, on the left bank of the Drino river, it gives the town a special beauty. The fortress is defended by 7 towers. It was reconstructed in 1811 - 1812 by Ali Pasha Tepelena. At this time an aquaduct (10 km) long, was constructed to bring in 28,000 gallons of drinking water a day from mount Sopot. It was demolished under the Sogu regime in 1932, and its stones used as building material. The fortress is in excellent condition. At the main entrance to the fortress is the national museum of arms, which tells the story of Albanian weapons through the ages. The first floor covers the period from neolithic times to independence, in 1912.

The second floor, includes the later period. Here, is a prison used as such during World War II, by the Germans. Among many Albanian's who were persecuted during that time, are two Albanian women (from Gjirokastra) Bule Naipi and Persefoni Kokedhima, whose statues are in front of the hotel.

The fortress has an open air theatre, where every 5 years are organized national festivals. 2,000 singers, dancers and musicians take part, one group from each of the 26 districts. Each group presents a sequence of songs, dances and instrumental pieces lasting 40 minutes and various prizes are awarded at the end. The music in southern Albania (south of Shkumbini river) is polyphonic, the songs often incorporating an intriguing vocal drone.

The music of northern Albania is all homophonic and yet, each region has its own distinctive flavour. The men hurl their voices as if from mountain to mountain, singing of brave heroes of the past, wars and hardships and their deep love for their homeland. The women sing of more domestic themes, of family traditions and festivals, harvests and weddings, spinning and weaving and in particular the haunting sorrows of exile.

According to the foreigners who have participated in these festivals, "Albanian's are natural artists and seemingly without any trace of nervousness and give exciting performances full of verve and energy".

We hope that this joyful pride and expertise in our folk culture will not be diminished in the future, with the changes towards a more western style of life.

Near to the open air theatre is displayed an American aeroplane, which is a "big enigma" to the tourists. Despite the photo prohibition mark on the plane, nearly all the visitors used to take pictures of it. The plane is a witness of the "cold war" between east and west, which reached its culmination in the '60-s. In 1957, the Albanian military forces, forced this American "spy plane" to land, while flying over the Albanian territory. The two American pilots were released back to the U.S.A. while the plane was kept as a witness to the victories of socialism over capitalism.

In the programs of "Albtourist" travel agency, there is included the visit to "Enver Hoxha's house", turned into a museum of the nation liberation war for the district. Here the tourists are introduced with the life and the political activity of Enver Hoxha, who was born in Gjirokastra, in 1908 and died in April 11, 1985 (by diabetes). In the centre of the town was erected the statue of Enver Hoxha, which was toppled down by the people of Gjirokastra, in 1991.

Ethnographical Museum : is a typical house of 3 storeys. The interior of the house are richly ornamented; the fireplaces are covered with plaster and decorated with plant and fruit motifs, while the ceiling and divans are made of carved wood. This museum gives a complete impression of the traditions and culture of the district.

In Gjirokastra, is an obelisk dedicated to the pioneers of education who struggled for national independence during the National Renaissance at the turn of the century.

The Mosque : was built in 1757. It has a circled stony roof and a tall minaret. This mosque is under reconstruction.

Tourists can be accommodated at "Cajupi" hotel (it is called so, in honour of the poet A.Z Cajupi who was born in Gjirokastra). The Hotel is not of a high quality, but as the town is so attractive the tourists do not mind spending the night in Gjirokastra. The hotel has a bar on the ground floor, with beautifully decorated ceiling and walls and wooden divans. There is a band playing Albanian folk music and foreign. There is a souvenir shop in the first floor and two dining rooms. They cook a characteristic local dish called - hoshaf (made of junket and figs). Gjirokastra is famous for the cheese and yoghurt.

Not all the rooms of this hotel have shower and toilets. Such a thing causes dissatisfaction on the part of the tourists, who are not completely prepared to encounter such problems.

*Gjirokastra reminds us of many funny stories with foreign tourists. One of which, is related to a British group which had only one Irish (who kept the group always in high spirits). Having finished with the distribution of the keys, the guides announced the dinner time. Everybody was excited to see whether his or her room was with a shower and toilet.*

*When the tourists came down to dinner, the Irish approached the guides, complaining about his coloured T.V. in his room that was not working properly : "I want my T.V mended at once!" - he demanded.*
*The rest of the group was shocked.*

*"Did you say you have a coloured T.V. in your room?" - asked an old lady.*

*"Yes, I did - retorted the Irish - I hope there is something wrong with the aerial As for the rest I am quite satisfied."*

*"What do you mean by "the rest"?*

*"Well, there is a bath - tub, a toilet, the floor is covered with a persian carpet, there is a fridge and the loveliest of all, is a fish aquarium. Perhaps, it is one of the rooms used for VIP-s".*

*"It is unbelievable, you have so many luxuries while we don't have even a toilet. This is not fair - concluded the old lady in despair".*

*"Why is the Irish privileged - asked one of the tourists - or is it because he has been to Albania twice and is friend to the guides?!!"*

"I am a bit surprised too - stated the guide - I don't know any room as described here."

"Why don't we go and see his room then? - suggested a grey haired British with a frowned face."

Most of the curious people from the group joined the guides and the boasting Irish leading the way to his room. But, to everybody's surprise, this room was on the ground floor, with iron bars in the window, no toilet, no shower, no T.V., nothing at all, except for the bed and a broken lampshade.

The room was invaded by a broad laughter of the people present. We didn't see the point of laughing; was it because the rest of the group realised there was no luxurious room in this hotel, or because the Irish's room was the same as theirs!? The same evening the Irish gentleman (who usually spent most part of the night drinking in the bar), asked the guide :

-"Would you please be so kind and knock at my door tomorrow at 5 a.m, as I have left my alarm clock at home?"

Next morning the guide forgot to wake him up and came downstairs to find the Irish having breakfast at the dining - room.

- "Thanks a lot for waking me up - he said to the guide with a smiling face. then he added to the group :

- "Albtourist had arranged a cock crowing at my window early this morning! It is an excellent "Albanian alarm -clock! As you see, Albtourist, is doing its utmost for me to enjoy myself in Gjirokastra, giving the best room and arranging cocks to crow early in the morning for waking me up!"

Soon, there is going to be built a new hotel in Gjirokastra, and we hope the tourists will not have any of such stories to tell.

There we were, two Albanian's, sharing fun and joys with these excellent people coming from the west, trying to enter their serene and joyful company. But there was always a bitter experience to remind us of the "strict moral code" of the system we were living *in, and then we felt sad, fearful, the smile freezing on our faces, a silent rage growing inside, endless "whys" and "whats" torturing our minds. We could easily notice the difference between the western people and the native; the former having freedom of speech while the latter shut in a suffocating shell of "rigid rules". We were witness in a manipulated court, threatened by a powerful jury, which dictated the testimony to us, while we were in silence supporting the "accused".*

*Many Albanian's were victims of the carefully weaved web of the system. One of the victims is an "Albtourist" driver, who being discovered to have an affair with one of the women in the group, was immediately given the sack. He was left jobless for more than 3 months and finding no other way out of his desperate situation, he decided to leave the country. But, he never managed to escape, as he was shot dead by the Albanian soldiers at the border. He payed with his life for infringing "the moral code",*

*Any time we look back at the past, we recall this bitter story with pain in our hearts.*

Departing from Gjirokastra and looking at the stony roofs, we recall what a foreign visitor once said : "I don't think there could be found another city in the world to match Gjirokastra. It seems as if, it were the kingdom of the fairy of the earth. A kingdom somewhat tired and veiled with a thin layer of haze".

On the way to Saranda, you traverse the plain of Dropulli (on the right side) where the are situated small villages inhabited by Greek minority. There are about 50,000 Greeks living in south and south east. They have the same rights as the rest of the population; the right to elect and to be elected, they are taught in their mother tongue, Greek language; there is a High Institute in Gjirokastra training teachers of Greek language; a daily newspaper in Greek language comes out regularly, called, "Laiko Vima" (People's Voice) and a daily programme in Radio "Tirana" in Greek language. There was created a Party called "Homonia", representing the Greek minority, which has a few seats in the parliament.

Climbing Muzina pass (570 m above sea level) and leaving

behind Kakavija, which is a frontier post on the border with Greece, on the opposite side, on the slope of the mountain you can see the village of "Glina" (where the "Glina" mineral water is extracted).

Not far from Muzina pass, on the right, is a small road, which leads to a salt mine, (the only salt mine in Albania). Further on, can be seen the artificial lake of the two Bistrica hydropower stations, built on Bistrica river. Down the hill is a wonderful spot, called "the blue eye" (Syri i kalter), formed by the underground springs. Sometimes tourists organize lunch picnics at this attractive site.

16 km away from Saranda, is situated the village of Delvina, which grew up around a fortress built on the hill in the eleventh and twelfth centuries. This area was captured by Ali Pasha Tepelena in 1811.

Delvina has a wood-working plant noted for its furniture and a factory for the processing of food and vegetables and for the production of alcoholic drinks, especially, wine.

At the village of Mesopotam, on the left of the road, there is a eleventh century church, which is quite remarkable for its architecture. The church was constructed by order of Constantine eleventh (1042 -1054).

The church of Mesopotam is under reconstruction and soon it will be functioning. It is needed to build at least a small bridge across the stream flowing by, to make the road accessible.

10km away from Saranda, on the right, rises the Finiqi hill. On its upper most part, once stood the city of Phoinike. Phoinike was the capital of the state of Epirus. During the period of the greatest expansion of the kingdom of the Ardian Illyrians, the city was occupied by the latter.

The city became rich, well fortified, by the fifth century B.C. and continued as such until the early Middle Ages. In Finiq, still stands a wall 7 metres high, forming a complex of zig-zag with gates and towers. During the excavations carried out here, various monuments, a thesaurus - a beautiful structure for keeping a treasury in, built in the forth century B.C., a water deposit of a later date and a number of sculptures were unearthed, some of which are displayed at the museum of Butrint. Before arriving in Saranda, on the right, there is a fish farm.

*SARANDA* : Near Saranda stood the ancient Illyrian city of Onchesmos, mentioned as a port in the first century B.C. In the forth century A.d. the town was fortified with walls. Inside the walls have been excavated the remains of dwellings,

water cisterns and an early Christian Basilica of the fifth and sixth century, containing a beautiful multicolored floor mosaic. Other mosaics are to be found in the district museum. The ruins are also preserved of an early Christian Monastery, of the "40 Saints", from which the modern name of the town (Saranda) is derived.

Saranda is situated in an open sea gulf, opposite the island of Corfu. The sea panorama, the variety of flora, favoured by the soft climate, make Saranda the preferred centre for rest and recreation and an important tourist town. Most Albanian couples come to spend their honey-moon in Saranda. That's why it is known in Albania as the town of the "honey-mooners".

Visitors can spend the night at "Butrinti" hotel. The hotel has a bar, a dining room and a souvenir shop (to the right). There is a nice veranda facing the sea, which are crowded during summer time. There is a taverna on the ground floor, which opens at 11 p.m. Here you are offered various drinks and there is a band playing southern Albania music.

Saranda has a disco where you can spend the evenings. There are also some restaurants in the town which close at 10.30 p.m.

*What to visit;*

Butrint : A picturesque road links Saranda with the archaeological centre of Butrint. Near Saranda, in the direction of Butrint, there is a new hotel, where locals spend their summer vacations.

Driving towards Ksamil, on the right side of the road lies the Ionian sea and on the left, the lake of Butrint. This lake feeds into the sea, through a channel called Vivari.

Because of this connection with the sea, the water of the lake is half salt and half sweet. The lake of Butrint (known in ancient times as Pelos) is rich in mussels; there are built wooden structures in the lake to catch the mussels.

The road passes by the peninsula of Ksamil, once a forlorn rocky pasture land, which is transformed into a huge orchard of citrus trees and subtropical plants. On top of a hill overlooking the sea, stands a nice two storeyed restaurant, which is preferred for its delicious meals (they usually serve trout, mussels, fish soup and a traditional cake called "shendetlie", made of honey, butter & flour). There is a semicircle terrace in front of the restaurant, from where, you have a clear view of the sea and the island of Corfu, which is only 4 km away.

Despite the rocky beach, the tourists prefer to swim in Ksamil, because of its crystal clear water.

There is a regular ferry, coming from Corfu to Saranda, twice daily. Tourists come on a one day trip from Corfu to Saranda. They visit Butrint, have lunch at the hotel, where they are entertained with music, and go back at 5 o'clock in the afternoon.

Leaving Ksamil, you drive to Butrint. The ancient city of Butrint has become today a much visited archaeological centre, where antiquity and beauty of nature intertwine. According to Virgil, Butrint (Buthroton) was founded by the Trojans during their voyage to Italy, but legends do not coincide with the archaeological records.

During the first millennium B.C., Butrint was a fortified centre of the Kaonian Illyrians, one of the big tribes of southern Illyria. But according to discoveries made in the area, it has been proved that the site was inhabited as early as the Palaeolithic period. In the sixth century B.C Greeks from Corfu settled here, alongside with Illyrians and the new colony grew and prospered as the result of trade, especially, in cattle, sheep and goats. By the fifth century B.C Buthroton was an Illyrian fortified city. In the third century B.C. the city was extended on to the plain south of the hill. At this time and even more in the second century B.C. a chain of public and private buildings were erected. In the forth century B.C, Butrint (Buthroton) had fallen to Epirus, and in 167 B.C. it was taken by Rome. It retained its autonomy for a time, but became a roman colony in 44 B.C. During this time, roman landowners settled in and around the city, which began to mint its own coins.

Under the rule of Byzantium, Butrint (as it is now called) continued to preserve its importance as a diocese centre. Butrint was captured by the Normans (eleventh century) and passed to Venice from 1690 to 1797, when is was captured by Ali Pasha Tepelena. With the fall of the Pashalik of Janina, in 1822, Butrint passed under Ottoman rule until 1913.

The first excavations were made here by an Italian archaeological mission, in 1927 - 1940 and after liberation there were a number of Albanian archaeologists, who continued the excavations.

The Excavations and the Monuments of Butrint : Approaching the archaeological site from the west, you will notice first two small fortresses and a hunting tower, built in the eighteenth century on the orders of Ali Pasha Tepelena.

The Temple of Asclepios : dedicated to the God of medicine and built in the second century A.D. on the foundations of an earlier structure. It consists of a covered portico and an inner chamber. The temple was connected with the theatre that stood next to it.

The Theatre : was built at the beginning of the third century B.C. It has 19 tiers of seats, running around the curve of the hill, the first tier having special seats for the nobels of the city. In the semicircular orchestra is an altar to Dionysos. The background to the stage consisted of a high wall, containing niches for works of sculpture. Here was discovered the so called Goddess of Butrint - in fact it is the head of a statue of Apollo stuck on the body of a woman. It was returned recently to Albania from Italy and now is to be found in the museum of national history in Tirana.

Close to the theatre is the public bath, the largest building so far excavated at Butrint. One of its rooms, the frigidarium, is paved with black and white mosaic stones, arranged in geometrical patterns.

To the east of the theatre are the remains of a roman dwelling house of the atrium type and beyond it some roman shops have been unearthed. To the south-east of these shops stand two - storeyed warehouses, crowned with vaults, and to the east of the shops a church of the early Middle Ages converted from a Roman temple.

To the east of the warehouses is the Baptistery, built in the mid eleventh century, which is one of the most beautiful examples of early Christian architecture in Albania. Its Baptismal room is circular, with a double row of granite pillars and a baptismal font in the centre. Its floor is decorated with 67 medallions of multicolored mosaics, which form 7 concentric circles : 5 of these have geometrical figures and plants motifs; in the other, two birds and animals are depicted. In order to protect the mosaics from the atmospheric agents, the archaeologists have covered them with sand. Only a small part of the mosaic is left uncovered to be seen by visitors.

Adjacent to the Baptistery are the remains of a thermal bath of which only the drainage system has been preserved, and of Nyphaion, a fountain dedicated to the Nymphs, dating from the beginning of the second century A.D.

Beyond the fountain, visitors reach the high walls of a basilica, built in the mid forth century. It is constructed of stone with big arches over the windows, and was originally covered with a wooden roof.

Close to the basilica are the remains of the walls, that surrounded the Acropolis. Of the former 6 gates to the city only 3 have been preserved. The Southern Gate of the town is reinforced by two towers. Northwards is the Main Gate. Not far from the Big Gate, there is another much smaller gate - the Lion's Gate - so called from a belief which portrays an encounter between a lion and a bull. From here steps lead up to a Well dedicated to the nymphs.

Climbing the hill one reaches the Butrint Museum, which is entered through a portico. Here are exhibited the objects excavated at Butrint in recent years. The exhibits of the museum complete the information gathered during the visit of the monuments.

After leaving the museum you find yourselves at the square in front of the fortress, which was reconstructed in the fourteenth century by the Venetian occupiers of the city. The visitor can admire the peaceful landscape of the lake and the mountains and hills that surround it, the channel that winds its way until it flows into the sea and the island of Corfu in the background. In forefront is the beautiful plain of Vrina, which stretches as far away as the hills.

Opposite Butrint, on the banks of the channel, is the fishing farm of Vavari.

If you are interested in detailed information on Butrint, you may refer to the book "Buthroti" published in 1987 in Albania. The book is translated in English.

After the visit to Butrint and lunch at Ksamil, you drive back to Saranda, where tourists usually spend 2 nights.

The most preferred place at the hotel is the taverna, which sometimes is crowded with tourists from different nationalities and perhaps it is the place where an affair can start.

*There were once two British youngsters, who were looking forward to having a temporary girlfriend to make their holidays more comfortable.*

*After a long unsuccessful effort, they asked the guide (who happened to be a girl) :*

*- "We have explored the town, but the only thing we are missing is a girlfriend. Do you think you can arrange girlfriends for us?"*

*- The Guide : "Have you consulted the Albtourist programme?"*

*- The English: "Yes we have, but there is nothing there about this!"*

*- The Guide: "Do you expect Albtourist to arrange even girlfriends for the people in the group?!!"*

*- The English :"No, no, ... but ... you know... Would you join us for a drink in taverna?"*

*- The Guide: "Yes, with pleasure."*

*As we had taken the seats in taverna with six other people from the group, one of them asked :*

*- "This morning at a factory we came across this slogan : - DISKUTIM; VENDIM; AKSION; - would you please translate it for us?"*

*- The Guide : "Diskutim means (Discussion) ; Vendim means (Decision), and Aksion (Action). It means that workers first discuss problems then decide upon them and in the end they act."*

*At this time a pretty German lady (who had come with a group of students from Berlin) entered the taverna.*

*- The English looking attentively at the German lady stated : "We have been - DISKUTIM - all the time in Albania; now its time for - VENDIM - and - AKSION- !!!"*

*After this solemn "Decision", he went to the German lady. Next morning, the group asked him whether he had enjoyed the time with the German.*

*- "No - answered he in despair - after having a bottle of wine, she claimed to have a boyfriend waiting for her upstairs. I think, it was not the fault of the German lady, neither it was my fault, it is the fault of the system of this country that stimulates only - DISKUTIM, DISKUTIM, DISKUTIM, NEVER - VENDIM and AKSION."*

*As you know, dear readers, there are different ways and means to express one's desire to a lady. One, may find it easier to be straightforward in his request; another expresses himself in a more refined way, which sometimes produces laughter;*

*Once, there was a group of Albanian students in a taverna, enjoying the time by telling fortunes. The soothsayer, (a pretty Albanian lady), asked a tourist if he was interested to know his fortune. After listening attentively to what the soothsayer told him, the tourist concluded boastfully :*

*- "You spent a long time telling my fortune and you used so many playing - cards. Now, I will tell your fortune, by using only three playing - cards!"*

*He picked up three cards from the pile and looking at them attentively, addressed himself:*

*- "Oh, what a lucky woman you are!! this evening, you will meet someone by chance and fall in love with him. He seems to be very handsome and he loves you too! After having a couple of drinks with him, you will go to room number - 405 -*

*- The lady was bewildered : "Who might this person be??"*

*- "Don't worry young lady, that person is sitting right in front of you, telling your fortune, and if you don't believe, here is the key to - 405 -We all enjoyed the subtle humour of the tourist.*

Departing from Saranda towards Vlora means an early start as Vlora is a long distance by car or coach (124 km).

The road passes through different villages along the seashore, lined with gardens and terraces of olive and citrus trees. Riviera, (coastroad) is one of the most beautiful routes in Albania. Many tourists have referred to the Riviera as "the Albanian pearl".

Riviera stretches along the foot of a range of mountains, which rise sharply from the sea to an altitude of 800 - 2000 above sea level. Fascinating, are the contrasts of nature and the rich vegetation by the seashore.

*LUKOVA* : is the first large village you come to, specialising in the cultivation of citrus fruits and olives and breeding cattle.

Otherwise, Lukova, is known as the village of the youth, as hundreds of students use to come to Lukova and work in the plantations, one month in a year. This was considered as a "Voluntary labour" and was included in the schooling programs of the secondary schools and the University.

Now, with the democratic changes in the country, this "voluntary labour" does not exist any more.

*Not far from Lukova, is a prison, which we visited once with a group of tourists. It was dark and misty. We were all tired, especially, the driver, who had been driving from Vlora to Saranda with lots of photo-stops on the way. The crossing near the prison, confused him and he took the wrong way, which lead up to a big iron gate surrounded by a long fence of barbed wire. A soldier, standing in front of the gate, pointed his machine gun to us. We were staring with our mouth wide open and here and there the bus was filled with long frightful interjections. this tense atmosphere was engraved by a strong, indignant voice, coming from the back of the bus :*

- *"What mistake have we done, that you are sending us to prison?!!!"*

- *"No, no dear tourist - answered we (trying to change the tense atmosphere into a comic one). - you haven't made any mistake. But, as you were tired, the driver wanted you to relax in prison!!"*

*The whole group burst into laughter.*

*This was not the only prison in Albania. There were other prisons in different regions, used for political reasons and ordinary ones.*

*According to the international Helsinki Federation Human Rights monitoring group, Albania had political prisoners, including some whose only crime was to try to emigrate.*

*In a meeting Christine von Kol a member of the Helsinki Delegation, pointed out:*

*- "It is unbelievable how prisoners are treated in Albania!"*

*But, what do we, Albanian's feel about this?*

*We are told there were prisoners who burned themselves or cut their arms deliberately, in order to escape from the inhuman work at the mines of Spac. At the alms house in Shkodra, we met an old man, with a pale bony face, marked with lines of old age. His toothless mouth wide open staring at the visitors.*

*-"He cant walk! - stated one of the nurses, all day he does nothing but cry! He has been to Spac prison for 15 years. His wife divorced him while he was in prison, as she was afraid they could send her in exile."*

*- "Ask him , how he feels? asked one of the British journalists that was with us.*

*We never got an answer, but a faint sobbing, coming from an exhausted soul.*

*Was he weeping because of his past? or perhaps his present? or ... perhaps, both.*

*We left the alms house with tears in our eyes. Despair over whelmed us all!*

Leaving Lukova, you drive towards the village of Borsh. Borsh, stands on the slopes of the mountains that come down to the very sea. The place has many cold and clear water springs, which make an attractive tourist centre.

There is another village on the seashore, somewhat different from the others, because it is situated upon a rock in a mountain gorge, and is called Qeparo. Between Qeparo and Himara village, there is a very picturesque gulf, the gulf of Porto Palermo - the ancient Panormon. It has been a small seaport, frequented by seamen in the Middle Ages. There is a small fortress erected by Ali Pasha Tepelena.

Another village you drive though is Himara, situated on a hill in the centre of the Albanian Riviera, 72 km away from Vlora. On the top of the hill are ruins of an Illyrian fortress, the ancient Chimera. This region has a history full of wars and heroic deeds, especially during the protracted encounters and uprisings against the Ottoman invaders. In some documents and records of the past, Himara is mentioned as the main centre of the region. In the Middles Ages, Himara was a centre of a diocese. The people of Himara have given a valuable contribution to the National - liberation War, fighting heroically against the Italian and German invaders. In Himara, there is a small bar, where you usually have a coffee break.

Leaving Himara behind, you drive to Vuno. It is one of the rather large villages of the seashore. The village was the scene of heavy fighting during the war and the village itself was razed to the ground, but was rebuild preserving its former aspect and characteristics.

Dhermi is another village in the Albanian Riviera. Deep in the mountains nestles the tiny church of St. mary, a church with interesting Medieval wall paintings. Dhermi, with its sandy beach, has become a popular holiday resort, where there is built a trade union hotel.

Stretching on both sides of a deep ravine, at the foot of mount Cika, Dhermi has a magnificent panorama.

Before climbing the Llogara Pass, there is the village of Palasa. It was here, in the gulf of ancient Palesta, that Ceasar landed his armies in the 48 B.C. to face those of Pompey and it was after climbing the Llogara Pass, that his march against his enemy began.

From here, the road begins to snake up, towards the Llogara Pass, the highest point of which if 1025 metres above sea level. Here quite a different landscape meets the traveller's gaze.

The traveller gets a tremendous view of the ionian sea, with the characteristic dark blue colour of its waters. The Ionian sea, differs from the Adriatic. While the depth of the Adriatic in the area between Shenjin and Bari is 1,590 metres, the depth of the Ionian sea reaches down to 4,594 metres, equal to the greatest depth of the Mediterranean basin. Along the Albanian seashore, the Adriatic is quite shallow : 50 km from the shore this depth does not exceed 100 metres. In the Ionian sea this depth is reached much nearer to the seashore.

Descending the Llogara Pass, the pine trees grow taller and taller and their pungent aroma becomes more intense. In the hot summer time, a refreshing coolness permeates the valley. All along the road, there are springs of ice cold water. In Llogara, there is a mountain health resort, where people can spend their holidays.

The distance from Llogara to Vlora is 39 km. Before arriving in Vlora you pass through the village of Orikum. The ancient city of Orikum was founded in the forth century B.C. during the period of the Ottoman occupation, it was known by the name of Pashaliman. The most important cultural monument remaining in the ancient fortress city, is the first century B.C. theatre with seats up to 500 spectators. There are also remains of dwellings, streets and water cisterns. Near by, are the ruins of the twelfth century church of Marmiro, built in the shape of a cross with a cupola.

*KANINA* : this village has been a dwelling site since the first half the last millennium B.C. by the forth century B.C it had become a fortified city. The defence's of the city were strengthened after the fall of Apollonia, when Vlora replaced it as a port. It is mentioned under its present name in documents of the forth century A.D. The fortress still stands on a hilltop. The city passed from Byzantine rule through various hands until conquered by the Turks in 1417. In the thirteenth century, by which time it had declined into a mere village, it was the seat of a bishopric.

At the entrance of Vlora, you pass through a picturesque resort centre of Uji i Ftohte (Cold Water). It is noted for its springs of cold water. These supply the town of Vlora with much if its drinking water, and pipes also feed large tanks in the middle of the bay of Vlora for the supply of ships.

Far to the left you can see the only inhabited island in our country, Sazan. Sazan is the largest island in Albania. It has a strategic position.

Sazan was known as early as the forth century B.C. under the name of Sason. It was for a long period under Venetian control, then taken in the forth century by the Ottoman Turks. At the beginning of the nineteenth century, the island was seized by Britain and passed in 1864 to Greece. In 1914, during the first World War, Italy occupied the island and retained control of it. In September 1943, following the surrender of Italy in the second World War it was occupied by German Troops. It was liberated by Albanian forces in October 1944.

Karaburun is the largest peninsula in Albania, stretching north-westwards to make the bay of Vlora into a natural harbour. It is 22 km long and 6 km wide.

*VLORA;* is proclaimed a "hero city". It is an old city, where important events in the struggles for freedom and independence have taken place. In ancient times the city was known under the name of Aulon. At the beginning it was only a port. Aulon was famous for its olive groves and vineyards.

After the fall of Apollonia and Orichum, it became the principal port of Illyria.

In the fifth century Aulon was the centre of diocese. The emigrations of barbarians damaged it badly and brought the withdrawal of the city deeper in land.

During the Middle Ages the city was fused into one with the fortress of Kanina, which is situated to the south east.

In 1081 Vlora was seized by the Normans and the German Hohenstaufens, and in 1272 incorporated into the kingdom of Arberia. In the fourteenth century, Byzantine armies visited it again, the Serbs as well as the feudal lords of the Balshas from north Albania.

At the fourteenth century, as it has passed to the Balshas, it became an important trading and handicraft centre noted apart from wines and salt, for its swords, its ships and its silk.

The invading Turks took it in 1417, and Sultan Sulejman "The Magnificent" built a fortress by the sea in 1531, which is believed to have been designed by the Albanian architect - Sinan.

By the seventeenth and eighteenth centuries, Vlora had again become an important economic centre and port. it was taken by Ali Pasha Tepelena in 1812.

It was in Vlora that an Assembly was convened, which proclaimed Albania as an independent state, forming the first national government headed by Ismail Qemali on the 28th of November, 1912. At this time Vlora became the capital of the country. The government remained there until January, 1914.

Vlora was occupied by the Italian troops in 1914 during the first World War, but they were driven from the main land in 1920, by a volunteer army. Reoccupied by Italians in 1939, and by the Germans in 1943. Vlora was liberated in October 15,-1944.

Today Vlora has a population of 61,300. Vlora is Albania's second largest port, it is also a fishing port and holiday resort.

*What to visit;*

The Mosque of Muradie, was built in 1542: this is believed to have been designed by the architect Sinani, on the orders of Sultan Sulejman, when he was in Vlora preparing his naval expedition against Italy.

With the closing down of the mosques and churches in 1967, it has been used as the museum of architecture of the district.

In the town centre is the bronze monument of independence, unveiled in 1972. On a high irregular pillar of rock stands a figure of a standard bearer, while below are depicted distinguished figures of the movement of Albania's independence. It is a joined work of the sculptors, Kristaq Rama, Shaban Haderi and Muntaz Dhrami. In honour of the day of independence, the main square in Vlora is called "The Square of the Flag" ("Sheshi i Flamurit").

The Museum of the Town, is a small historic and ethnographic museum, where through the exhibits, one is acquainted with the history and ethnographic peculiarities of the region.

The ethnographic section, with its exhibits, shows the ethnographic wealth and variety of the region.

To be mentioned is the men's folk dress, which is typical for the southern regions. The men wear a white wide skirt known as, fustanella, and low heeled leather shoes, known as, opinga (decorated with a tassel). These dresses are usually worn in the folk festivals for other festivities.

The Museum of Independence : reflects the stern struggle of the Albanian's for freedom and independence, the events that brought about the raising of the flag on the 28th November 1912, when Albania was proclaimed an independent state.

Vlora has a cement factory, soda and P.V.C. works, electric lamp factory, factories for dehusking of rice, for the extraction of Tannin, and the production of plastics, there is a cannery, whose products are used for export. The region of Vlora is rich in agricultural products, especially in fruits, olives and grapes, and in dairy products.

Vlora is the seat of the higher school for naval officers, opened in 1961, which trains officers not only for the navy, but for the merchant and fishing fleets. Also a high military school of aviation, opened in 1962, which trains personnel for the air force. Boys from 18 - 27 years old, join the army. Soldiers wear green uniforms. In 1966, copying the Chinese model of the army, the ranks were abolished, to be re-established in 1991.

Vlora has a secondary medical polytechnic school. After graduating from this school, the students have the right to attend the Medical Faculty in Tirana, for 5 years. Some of the doctors are sent to other countries, especially, Italy and France to attend training courses.

Compared to the past the medical service in the country has improved. Diseases such as malaria, cholera, smallpox, tuberculosis and syphilis, which were widespread, have virtually been eliminated, and the average expectation of life has risen from 38 to 69 years. In 1938, there was only one doctor for every 8,573 of the population, today there is one doctor for every 573 people. there are 4,000 dental clinics and 772 hospitals all over the country. There are 765 maternity hospitals and wards, in which 86% of babies are born. Pregnant women receive 6 months paid maternity leave. A nursing mother is entitled a leave from absence, with without loss of pay to feed her baby; a mother is entitled to paid leave if her child is ill. Labour legislation exists to protect the health and safety of workers.

Economic crises that have captured Albania lately, have influenced the medical system as well. The funds for this important section of life decreased, paralysing sometimes the normal work of the nurses and the doctors. Nevertheless, it is only a temporary situation which will improve in the future.

Lunch can be taken in a nice spot on the top of a hill, called "Kusbaba", from where you have a whole view of Vlora. After leaving Vlora the 5 km a road goes off on the left to Narta. The Narta lagoon was formerly linked with the sea by three canals separated by two rocky hills, but two of these are now silted up, leaving only the most northerly of the three, still open. The lagoon of Narta is a large salt lake, in an area of 34 square kilometres. It has a very high salt content, and has been used as a source of salt since the Middle Ages. Narta was an ancient settlement under the name of Arta, noted for its excellent wines and tasty fish.

Leaving the Narta lagoon, just before the village of Novosela, the road and railway cross the river Vjosa on Milfol Bridge (Ura e Mifolit). In ancient times this was a staging point on the road between Apollonia and Aulon.

The channel from the Vjosa to the large village of Levan, to which you now come, was the first stage in the draining of the marshland of the Myzeqe area, through which the road has been running for some kilometres. The district takes its name from the great Muzakaj family, which held it from the thirteenth to the end of the fifteenth century. The last of the Muzakajs, John, retired to Naples, where he published in 1510 his "Historia e Genealogia della Casa Musaccia", a work of great value for the history of Albania.

Later, you pass the village of Cakran, where important discoveries of prehistoric material (implements of flint, bone and horn, millstones, pottery kiln, and pottery, underground dwelling, burials) have been made. The site is dated to the Middle Neolithic. Here too was discovered in 1978 a hoard of 2500 coins from Apollonia, Dyrrachium, Oricum and elsewhere. After passing the chemical fertilisers factory and a thermo-electric power station (the largest in Albania) you drive to the right, towards the town of Berat.

The road comes to Roskovec, a large village noted for the quality of its tobacco. At the hamlet of Poshnja, which has an old bridge, over the Osum, you turn left in the direction of Berat and in another 4 km cross, the Osum on the Oil Bridge (Ura Vajgurore), formerly known as Hassan Bey's Bridge (Ura e Hasan beut), and enter the Osum Valley. A side road goes off to Kucova, formerly called, Qytet Stalin, (Stalin Town), Albania's oldest oil town, where oil has been worked since 1922. The road to Qytet Stalin passes on the right the village of Perondi, which has a fine Byzantine church.

The main road continues to Berat, and leaving the textile factory on the left, you enter the museum town of Berat.

*BERAT* : The town of Berat, overshadowed to the east by mount Tomorr (2400m), is built on an ancient Illyrian dwelling site, which goes back to the sixth century B.C. Its innumerable monuments and beautiful and characteristic architecture of its houses have proclaimed Berat, a museum town.

During the second century B.C. the town was called Antipatrea. it was a strategic fortress of the Illyrian Dasaretes tribe. In the ninth century the town was captured by the Bulgarians, who held it until the eleventh century and renamed it, Beligrad (white City), from which the present name is derived. During the thirteenth century, it fell to Michael Angelus Comnenus, the despot of Epirus; in 1345 to the Serbs; and in 1450 to the Turks. After the Ottoman conquest it fell into decline, and at the end of the sixteenth century had only 710 houses. Berat began to revive in the seventeenth century, especially after an earthquake in 1851, becoming a craft centre, noted particularly for its artistic wood carving. In 1809, it was seized by Ali Pahsa Tepelena.

The town is composed of three parts : Gorica, on the far side of the river ; Mangalem, on the fortress side of the river; and the residential quarter within the fortress (known as Kalaja). The houses on the fortress side which date from the seventeenth century, have typically two storeys, with the upper storey slightly overhanging and rich wood carving within. With their wide facades and large windows, they seem to be built almost on top of one another, giving Berat its name of : "The town of a thousand windows".

Berat has a population of 37,000 inhabitants. The hills and the mountain slopes around Berat, are planted with fig trees olive trees and other fruits.

*What to visit :*

The Fortress, is built on a rocky hill on the left bank of the river Osum and is accessible only from the south. After being burned down by the Romans in 200 B.C. the walls were strengthened in the fifth century under Byzantine Emperor Theodhosius II, and were rebuilt during the sixth century under the Emperor Justinian and again in the thirteenth century under the Despot of Epirus, Michael Angelus Comnenus.

The main entrance, on the north side, is defended by a fortified courtyard and there are three smaller entrances.

The fortress of Berat in its present state, even though considerably damaged, remains a magnificent sight. The surface that it encompasses made it possible to house a considerable portion of the cities inhabitants. The buildings inside the fortress were built during the thirteenth century and because of their characteristic architecture are preserved as cultural monuments.

The population of the fortress was Christian, and it had about 20 churches (most built during the thirteenth century) and only one mosque, for the use of the turkish garrison, (of which there survives only a few ruins and the base of the minaret).

The churches of the fortress were damaged through years and only some have remained. The Church of St. Mary of Vllaherna dating from the thirteenth century, has sixteenth century mural paintings by Nikolla, son of the Albania's most famous medieval painter, Onfuri. In a small tree - planted square, on a hillside inside the walls of the fortress, stands the fourteenth century Church of the Holy Trinity. It is built in the form of a Greek cross and has Byzantine murals. Outside the ramparts is the Church of St. Michael (Shen Mehill), Built in the thirteenth century. This church is reached by a steep but perfectly safe path.

Near the entrance, after a guardhouse, is the little Church of St. Theodore (Shen Todher), which have wall paintings by Onufri himself.

The most interesting is the cathedral of St. Nicholas, which has been well restored and is now a museum dedicated to Onufri. Onufri was the greatest of the sixteenth century painters in Albania. Not only was he a master of the techniques of fresco and icons, but he was the first to introduce a new colour in painting, pink, which was considered by the French critics as Onufri's red. In addition, Onufri, introduced a certain realism and a degree of individuality in facial expression.

The first inscription recording Onufri's name was found in 1951, in the Shelqan church. The Kastoria church has a date 23 July 1547 and a reference to Onufri's origin : "Une jam Onufri, dhe vij nga qyteti i shkelqyer i Beratit" (I am Onufri, and come from the town of Berat). Onufri's style in painting was inherited by his son, Nikolla (Nicholas), though not so successful as his father. In Onufri's museum are to be found works of Onufri, his son, Nikolla and other painters'. There are also numbers of icons and some fine examples of religious silversmith's work (sacred vessels, icon casings, covers of Gospel books, etc). Berat Gospels, which date from the forth century, are copies (the originals are preserved in the National Archives in Tirana). The church itself has a magnificent iconostasis of carved wood, with two very fine icons of Christ and the mother of God. The bishop's throne and the pulpit are also of considerable quality.

After visiting the fortress, you may have coffee or other drinks at a nice two-storeyed bar (on the first floor is the restaurant), built in harmony with the characteristic architecture of Berati houses. From the veranda, on the second floor, you have a magnificent view of the town below. Sometimes, tourists prefer to have lunch at this restaurant. The parts of the town below the fortress have a larger Muslim population. There are a number of interesting buildings.

Near the street running down from the fortress is the Bachelors Mosque (Xhami e Beqareve), built in 1827. this has a handsome portico and an interesting external decoration of flowers, plants, houses, etc. The word "beqar", which literally means "bachelor", here refers to the young shop assistants (in practice generally bachelors), whom the merchants in Berat as the other towns - used as a kind of private militia.

The King's Mosque (Xhamia e Mbretit), the oldest in the town built in the reign of Bayazid II (1481 - 1512), is notable for its fine ceiling.

The Leaden Mosque (Xhamia e Plumbit), built in 1555 and so called from the covering of its cupola. This mosque is the centre of the town.

The Teqe of the Helveti (Teqe e Helvetive), of 1790, with a handsome porch and a carved and gilded ceiling.

As a result of the atheist policy propagated by the Albanian government, all these mosques, churches and other religious institutions were closed down in 1967. Religion went through a hard time. Religious propaganda, being considered as anti-state and subversive, was prohibited by law. Special attention was paid to the schooling programs, which were purged from any religious ideology. Students had no access at all, to religious literature. The Bible and Koran were fiercely criticised.

The churches and the mosques were looked at, as fossils coming from an ancient world. They were called with different names :"museum of art", "palace of sports", "architectural museum", "centre of cultural relations" etc, but never by their own name. As a matter of fact, sometimes, these architectural objects were transformed into warehouses.

The word "God" was considered as outdated, it was gradually extinguished from the Albanian dictionary. Instead of saying "for God's sake" (per hater te Zotit - a very popular phrase used in everyday speech), the communist propaganda induced the people to use the other phrase : "for the sake of Party's ideal" (per ideal te Partise), which became synonymous to the former.

Small children, felt ashamed of their grandparents, when they discovered them to be "silent believers of God" Sometimes, such a thing brought about open criticism on the part of nephews and nieces, trying to convince their grandparents, that God was non-existent. But it didn't always work like this; there were some grandparents, who gave to their children religious education. They organized religious ceremonies, at home secretly, kept symbols like, cross-necklace, prayed regularly, but never exposed themselves to public, as such a thing, was "a sin against socialism" and the sinners were persecuted.

It was only in 1991, that religion was legalized; all churches, mosques and other religious institutions, function regularly.

Beside religious buildings, Berat has also a seven - arched Bridge, built by Kurt Pasha in 1790, but now disfigured by modern parapets, which still gives access to the outlying quarter of Gorica, on the other side of Osum river.

Having visited the wonderful town of Berat, you can find accommodation at "Tommorri" hotel, which is at the centre of the town. Not all the rooms in the hotel have toilets and showers. There are collective toilets on each floor. There is a restaurant and a bar. At the reception, you may buy postcards and booklets with illustrations from the town of Berat. Soon, there is going to be built a new hotel, next to the existing one.

Next stop Tirana, to the capital of the country. On the way to Tirana, you pass through Lushnja, Kavaja and the beach area of Durres. The trip takes approximately, two and a half hours.

*TIRANA* ; was proclaimed as the capital of Albania in the year 1920 (at the Congress of Lushnja). According to some sources of information, it appears that the city was founded in the year 1614, by the feudal lord of that region, at that time Sulejman Pasha Mulleti in order to attract the population of the region to the new settlement, he built a mosque, a bath house and a bakery. According to Marin Barleti, people spoke of little Tirana and big Tirana not as settlements, but as plains. Tirana began to be developed as a town in the eighteenth century, noted for silk and cotton fabrics, leather, pottery and silverware. In the nineteenth century, Tirana fell to the Albanian feudal family of the Toptanis; and during the first Balkan war (1912 - 1913), it was temporarily occupied by Serbian troops. The ex-communist Party was founded in Tirana, on the 8th of November 1941. during the years 1939-1944, the Albanian people fought heroically against the fascist and nazi invaders, for the liberation of the country. The occupying forces finally abandoned the town on 17th November 1944 and the new government made its triumphal entry on the 28th November.

Today Tirana is the largest city in Albania, with a population of over 300,000 inhabitants, and is the political, economic and cultural centre.

*What to visit:*

At the centre of Tirana lies Scanderbeg's Square. In a garden, in the centre of the square, stands the bronze equestrian statue of Gjergj Kastrioti - Scanderbeg, unveiled in 1968. It stands on a low pedestal of large limestone blocks, and portrays the national hero setting out to war, holding his sword in his right hand, while his left hand holds the reins of the horse. On the eastern side of the square stands the Palace of Culture, the largest cultural building in the country. Its construction was

begun in 1960, on the site of capital's old bazaar, and was opened in l966. It has an opera and ballet theatre; the opera and ballet company was formed in 1953, on the basis of the philharmonic (1950). Albania has 7 symphony orchestras, and there are 13 smaller orchestras attached to the variety theatres and more than 40 military bands. The Palace of Culture also contains the National Library. It has more than 860,000 books.

The Museum of National History (opened in 1981) is situated on the northern side of the square. The huge mosaic entitled "Albania" at the front, the largest in the country, symbolizes centuries-old history of the struggle of the Albanian people.

Leading eastward from Scanderberg's Square is "28 Nentori" (28 November) Street, on the corner of which stands the Mosque of Haxhi Ethem Bey. Its construction began in 1794 and was completed in 1823. Next to the mosque stands the Clock tower built in 1830, but reconstructed later. In a side street nearby is the People's theatre. In May 1944, on the eve of liberation, the first professional theatre in the history of

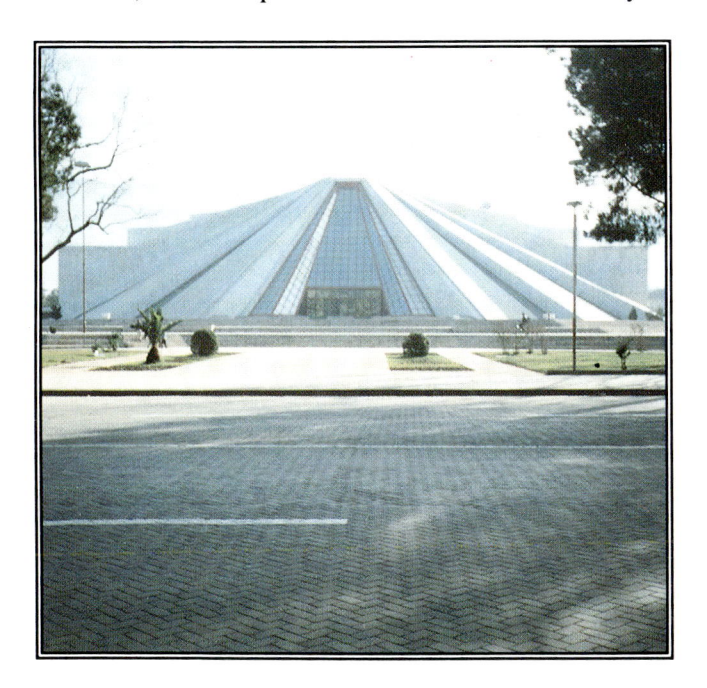

Albania was created in the liberated town of Permet. Today, the country has 10 professional drama companies, 15 variety theatre companies and 26 puppet theatre companies. In 1946 the first secondary school specializing in drama, the "Jordan Misja" lyceum, came into being and in 1959, the "Aleksander Moisiu" Higher School for Actors, was opened, to become later a department of the Higher Institute of Arts.

Leading west from the square is the Avenue of the "Peza Conference", on the corner of which stands the State Bank, established in 1945.

Northwest off the avenue of the "Peza Conference" is the "Durres Road" which leads to the airport. From the south of the square runs the Avenue of the Martyrs of Nation. This has ministerial buildings on both sides. On the left is the Art gallery, "Dajti" hotel, the ex-museum of "Enver Hoxha", now the Centre of International Cultural Relations, the Council of Ministers, the Palace of Congresses, the library of Tirana University, and Archaeological Museum. While on the right is : ex-building of the Central Committee of the PLA (now the Ministry of Finance, the residence of the Socialist Party and the Ministry of Jurisprudence). Further on is the Residence of the Parliament, the Higher Institute of Fine Arts, and in front, at the end of the road is Tirana University, set up in 1957. Today it has about 12,000 students. It has 8 faculties with 28 departments. there are a number of dormitories built up in Tirana (the area called student town) where the students from different districts of Albania are accommodated.

Behind the Tirana University is the Great Park of Tirana containing an artificial lake, an open-air theatre, a restaurant and a bar. There is also a botanical garden and a small zoo.

In the main avenue used to be the statues of Lenin and Stalin, which were pulled down in 1991. Behind the Palace of Congresses is "Qemal Stafa" stadium and the building of Albanian Radio TV Station. The first radio service in Albania was provided by a three kilowatt short-wave station in Tirana, which began broadcasting in November 1938. Regular radio programs began only on November 27, 1944, on the eve of liberation. Today the powerful transmitter of Radio Tirana broadcasts uninterruptedly in Albanian and in some foreign languages. (there used to be 22 foreign languages, now the number is reduced). There are also four local radio stations in Gjirokastra, Korca, Kukes and Shkodra.

*Berlin Restaurant*

The regular TV programs began in 1971. In 1981, transmission in colour began. There is a license fee payable for radio and TV. The programs on TV start at 12:00 p.m. till 23:00 p.m. In Tirana there is also the Albanian Telegraphic Agency (ATSH).

Running parallel with the avenue of the Martyrs of Nation, to the east is Elbasani Road, here is to be found the Academy of Sciences created in 1972. It has three sections concerned with natural sciences, technical sciences and social sciences and publishes a number of scientific journals.

On a low terraced hill, in the south-eastern district is laid out the cemetery of the Martyrs of the Nation where are buried about 900 men and women who fell in the War of National Liberation. The cemetery is overlooked by the giant statue "Mother Albania", 12 metres high. It symbolizes Albania as a mother; her right hand holding up a star and a laurel (symbols of International unity and peace), her left hand lying at her side to soothe the fallen. In front of the statue is written: "Everlasting Glory to the Martyrs of the Nation". A short distance from the cemetery on the other side of the road is the Brigades Palace, once the Royal Palace of King Zog. It now serves for official receptions.

Turning back to the centre of the town to the west, by the stream Lana, is the Ethnographical Museum. It has three pavilions, which reveal the rural and urban traditions in Albania. Tirana puts an end to the first itinerary.

# ITINERARY - TWO

ITINERARY - TWO.

TIRANA - ELBASAN - POGRADEC - KORCE - PERMET - TEPELENE - GJIROKASTER - SARANDE - DURRES

Every trip through Albania reveals something new. From an entirely mountainous landscape, the visitor after a short time finds himself on the plain's. After having travelled along a valley, all at once a wide horizon opens before his eyes. This time our trip deviates from the sea and goes towards the interior of the country.

After spending one night in Tirana you leave the capital and take a southeastern route, towards the very heart of Albania, to Elbasan. Hardly out of the capital the road begins to climb the range of hills overlooking Tirana. This is indeed a very picturesque road for tourists.

After having passed the Palace of Brigades (ex-King Zog's Residence), where government ceremonies are usually conducted, a new scenery with vineyards and fruit plantations, strikes one's eyes. You cross the Erzen river and find ourselves at the foot of hill on the top of which stands the fortress of Petrela.

This fortress was built in the late eleventh century with the purpose of defending the road that passed on to Durres. The fortress played an important role in the campaigns of Scanderbeg, forming a part of the defence system of the fortress of Kruja. It is said to have been the residence of the hero's sister, Mamica and to contain the grave of their contemporary Ballaban Pasha, an Albanian who went over to the Turks.

Leaving Petrela and having travelled along the river banks, the highway begins to ascent the mountain of Krraba. There is a coal mining centre at the village of Mushqeta and Gracan.

The road through the mountains of Krraba is very picturesque, it winds around and around from hill to hill and from mountain to mountain, revealing to the tourists a beautiful landscape along the valley of Erzen river. At the 20th km landmark you enter the district of Elbasan. To the south rises majestic the towering profile of Tomorri mountain, whereas to the southeast stretches Shkumbini river. Here the road begins to descend rapidly towards the plain of Elbasan.

On the northwest are the mountains of Krraba, whereas on the southeast one range of hills following another lead to the (Llixha) Spa - sulphurous hot springs of a temperature of 50'C.

On the right side there is the Metallurgical combine of Elbasan, which produces various kinds of steels, and at the same time causes a huge air pollution. This complex is of Chinese technology. Billions of leks were spent to make it work, but it has always been a burden on the weak shoulders of the Albanian economy, it has never proved to be profitable to date.

*ELBASAN* : is the site of the ancient city of Skampa founded in the first century A.D. It came into being and developed during the construction of the Egnatia route - a main road artery in the land communications and trade and commercial interchanges between the Apennine Peninsula, on one side and the Balkan Peninsula and the East on the other. The surrounding walls of the town were built in the forth century, having 3 entrances and 26 towers. its fortress was built during the reign of the Byzantine Emperor Justinian I (483-565) by which time Skampa had become the seat of a Bishopric with a Cathedral and a Basilica outside its surrounding walls. After the failure of the second Turkish siege of Kruja, Sultan Muhamet II rebuilt the fortress in 1466 and renamed the town Elbasan (El-basan is turkish for Fortress).

In the sixteenth and seventeenth centuries, Elbasan became an important centre of trade and handicrafts noted for its leather, wood, silk and metal work (especially silver). In the nineteenth century local feudal lords led an uprising against the Turks, who destroyed the walls of the fortress in 1832, so that only their southern part still stands. One of the gates of the fortress is still in use.

Beside the hotel "Skampa" is a bath-house of the Turkish period. A museum relating the history of the Elbasan district is located in the fortress. It's exhibits include the tombs of an Illyrian warrior, with helmet, arms and household utensils and two statues of Apollo. Today Elbasan has a population of 70,000 inhabitants, and it is Albania's fourth largest town and the administrative centre of a district. The town is the birthplace of the teacher Theodor Haxhi

Filipi known as Dhaskal Todri (1730-1805) and of the lexicographer Kostandin Kristoforidhi (1827-1895). In Elbasan was opened the first teachers training college (1909) the "Alexander Xhuvani" University, named after the poet and publicist.

*What to visit:*

The fortress of Elbasan is one of the monuments of the city that attracts the visitors' attention.

The Archaeological Museum : where there are exhibited various archaeological collections that narrate the history of the city and its surroundings. Of interest there are the archaeological materials that throw light on the culture of the Illyrian centre.

The Turkish Bathhouse : situated on the side of "Skampa" hotel.

Museum of the National-Liberation War and the Museum of Education.: Elbasan has a wood processing industrial combine, a factory for the processing and fermentation of tobacco, a big oil refinery has been set up not far from the city (Cerrik), a cement factory, engineering works and construction materials factory.

After the visit, you can enjoy a coffee break at "Skampa" hotel before the drive southeast towards the town of Pogradec.

The road to Pogradec leaves Elbasan to the East and follows the attractive valley of the river Shkumbin. This is the route of the ancient "Via Egnatia" along which passed many invading and conquering armies as well as trade caravans heading for the East and the West alike. It was along the Via Egnaita that the roman legions marched on their road to conquest towards the East. From the East on the other hand came the armies of Byzantium and the invaders like Goths and Bulgarians. During the eleventh and twelfth centuries, the Normans and later on the Crusaders marched over this very route coming from the sea. This route brought from the East the numerous armies of the Osman Sultans, intent on occupying Albania.

The road proceeds eastward through the village of Labinot. Here the river runs tranquilly in its bed, in marked contrast to its turbulence up in the mountains. A local legend tells that a shepherdess from Labinot was in love with a young shepherd from Polis, a hamlet just across the river, but the lovers were unable to speak to each other because they could not make themselves heard over the roar of the waters. The girl begged the river to be silent so that she could say a few words to her lover and from that day the waters have been calm.

The road proceeds through Librazhd, Qukes and Prrenjas. This area is rich in iron and iron nickel ores.

Leaving Prrenjas behind, you can see on the right of the plain of Domosdova. It is believed that it was on the plain of Domosdova that the first encounter took place between Albanian army lead by Scanderbeg and Turks in the year 1444, where the Albanian's defeated badly the invading army of the Ottoman Turks. It is said that the turks named the plain (Domosdove - meaning in Turkish -cursed land) after the loss they suffered.

The road snakes to Thana Pass (Qafe thana) 391m above sea level. On top of Thana Pass there is a crossing; the road to the left leads to Struga (16 kms long) and 4 kms away from the boarder line with Yugoslavia.

As you leave the Pass you can see below the Oher Lake. Oher Lake known in ancient times as Lacus Lychnidus, its the second largest lake in Albania. Although the borderlines partly with Yugoslavia it has a total area of 360 square m (140 square miles, 42 square miles within Albania). Its maximum depth is 286 metres. It is one of the deepest lakes in Balkans. The lake is noted for the purity and transparency of its water, which is the home of two unique and extremely tasty species of trout - the koran and the belushk. There are breeding stations for koran at Tushemisht (near Pogradec and Lin). The scenery with the Oher lake in front and the typical fisherman village, Lin, on the right is so attractive that one cannot help stopping the car and taking a picture of it.

At the top of a hill near this area are the remains of a Christian basilica built the end of the fifth century. It has rich multi-coloured mosaic with animal, plant and geometrical motifs.

On a clear day one can see on the left, the town of Struga and further on something of the town of Oher, both of them in Yugoslavia.

Before entering the town of Pogradec is the village of Guri i Kuq the underground of which is rich in iron nickel.

*POGRADEC*: On the top of the hill overlooking Pogradec there is an ancient Illyrian fortress believed to have been known as Encheleana. In the Middle Ages this fortress was reconstructed and the place was renamed by the Bulgarians, who invaded Southeastern Albania at this time. (Pogradec, Pod Grad - the place beneath the fortress ). During the Eighteenth century under Turkish occupation, the town became an administrative centre, but was largely destroyed ruing the World War I, again during the Italian-Greek War of 1940-1941 and twice during the National Liberation War (1941-1944); however a number of characteristic houses have been preserved as cultural monuments. Pogradec has a population of 15,000 inhabitants. It is a centre of the food industry, noted for its canned fruits, vegetables and dairy products. There are also factories producing furniture, tobacco and knitwear. Pogradec has an excellent bathing beach and has a great future as a tourist centre. The environment offers an alpine like scenery of rare beauty. The lofty mountains of Kamja and Guri i Topit stand over it like a crown.

You may have lunch either at the "Guri i Kuq" (red Stone) hotel in the town or at a nice spot not far from the lake, known as Drilon or Voloreka. Two characteristic restaurants, situated in a lovely park decorated with willow trees, and by streams flowing down to the lake, make the lunch stop unforgettable for the tourists. The park of Drilon is frequently visited by the Albanian's as well, who come to picnic. In Voloreka normally they cook fish-koran, which is famous for its delicious meat.

Speaking of fish, there is a recent joke about the communist fish in Albania? It happened once that a citizen went fishing in the lake. He waited for hours and in the end to his great fortune a little fish caught the hook. The fisherman sent the fish to his wife, who, to his big surprise, became nervous at the sight of the fish. "How do you expect me to cook the fish, when there is no stewpan, no cooking oil, Nothing?" Send it back to the lake, I can't cook it" Poor husband threw the fish back into the lake, which soon got its small mouth out of the water shouting happily; "Long live the Party of Labour! Long live socialism!"

The road towards Korca leaves Pogradec in a southeastern direction. Leaving the lake behind, it passes fields and vineyards. The road and the scenery are very attractive. The road passes through the small town of Maliq, which is 7 miles before reaching the town of Korca.

*MALIQ*: The new town of Maliq has been build on a site famous for its history, notable for its neolithic dwellings built on stilts.

Prior to liberation the whole area was a hugh marsh, and one of the first major post-Liberation projects was the draining of this marsh, which began in 1947. In 1951 the sugar refinery was set up, and this now forms part of the large sugar combine, which produces (in addition to sugar), alcohol, yeast, starch, glucose and carbon dioxide.

From Maliq to Korca the distance is 12 km. The boulevard you enter and the tall chimneys of various factories and workshops indicate that you have reached the town of Korca.

*KORCA* : is situated at the foot of the Morava mountains, on the slopes of St. Thana hill, it was an Illyrian settlement in ancient times. Later there was built near here the ancient city of Pelion, which was captured during the second Macedonian War with the roman Army under Sulpicius Galba in 199 B.C. By the early Middle Ages Korca had become an urban centre with a ninth century church, rebuilt in the fourteenth century. During this time, a mosque and a hamam were erected and the town developed quickly. The Mirahori mosque was built in 1418. Korca grew considerably in the seventeenth century, especially after the burning of Voskopoja. By this time, it had become a centre of carpet-making as well as a focal point for trade. From Korca caravans set off for all parts of Europe. A large bazaar was built, preserved as a cultural monument. The city has lived through difficult times especially at the beginning of the ninth century, which brought as a consequence the wholesale emigration of its inhabitants to Romania, Egypt and America. Korca was a pioneer in the field of education. The first school in the Albanian language was established here in the 7th of March 1887, (which remained open until the year 1902), and the first school for girls in the Albanian language in 1891.

Under the Ottoman occupation Albanian culture was suppressed. After independence in 1912, Albanian education developed to some extent, but was cut back under the Italian and German occupation (1944).

In 1946 education was made free and secular and a large-scale-scheme of evening classes was inaugurated to eliminate illiteracy in adults. In 1952, elementary education for seven years was made compulsory for all children, and 1963 this was extended to eight years from 6 - 14. Children under 6 years of age are sent to kindergartens. In isolated mountainous districts, where a locality doesn't have their minimum number of children, they are sent to boarding school, from which they return home every weekend.

After completing compulsory education, pupils have the right to attend the secondary schools for four years. Most secondary schools have a vocational character, training pupils for a particular occupation. Pupils with an average mark of 8 or more, were given the right to attend the University (the system of marks in Albania is from 1 to 10; from 1 to 4 if you fail). With the changes in the country, the University may be attended by everyone that passes the preliminary test. There used to be two weeks of military training each year for the secondary school pupils (3rd-4th years) and University students a thing which does not exist any more now. The lessons start at 8.00 a.m. till 1.30 p.m. (with short breaks between lessons). School starts on the 1st September till the end of June.

School vacations are as follows:

- Christmas vacations (end of December - 11th January)
- April 1-7 (elementary schools only)
- July and August (summer vacations).

Education at all levels is free (until now). The family pays only towards the cost of school meals and of text-books. A few pupils are given scholarships, especially those coming from large families, while the rest of the pupils have to cover the living expenses on their own.

Besides being an important schooling centre Korca has played its part in the long term struggle history. Korca was occupied by the Greek troops 1912-1914 and by French forces in 1916-1920. The latter set up the "autonomous republic of Korca" 1916-1918, which joined the rest of Albania, when the French withdrew in 1920. During the French occupation a Lyce was established in 1917. In 1940-1941, the town was again occupied by the Greek forces, during the war between Italy and Greece. At the beginning of the twentieth century Korca became an important centre of the movement for independence from Turkish rule, producing distinguished patriots, like Themistokli Germenji (1871 - 1917) and Mihal Grameno (1872-1931).

The population is 60,000 inhabitants. Korca is now an important agricultural and industrial centre. The first brewery in Albania was established here and is still in operation. The 'Petro Papi" instrument work (1969) produces machine tools and measuring instruments of high quality. The 8th of March carpet enterprise (1967) is the largest factory of its kind in the country, which produces carpets and rugs with a workforce composed mainly of women and girls. A lot of carpets and rugs are exported to other countries. Korca has an ancient tradition in making Kilims. Fullers were available everywhere to treat home-made textiles. Rough home spun was compacted in fulling-mills, while vats under a waterfall were used to make carpets and blankets, supply and slightly felted- either the plaf with long fibres, or the velenxe, with a mixture of goats' and sheeps' wool which produced thick blankets. The sexhade is a handknotted carpet, the technique of making which was learned in some parts of the country from carpets brought from the east and seen in Mosques. In home workshop, the knotted carpets are works horizontally. These products, in attractive colours are good imitations of Persian carpets and of excellent quality. Nearly every housewife had a handloom at home, with which she made multicolored woollen kilims. There are still houses in Korca that continue this beautiful tradition.

The knitwear combine, the agricultural machinery work (1962), the woodworking enterprise, the shoe and footwear factory (1946), the artistic products enterprise are some of the main enterprises in this town.

*What to visit:*

The most interesting visit is the Museum of Medieval Arts opened in l980; it covers a period from the 5th to the 19 century and there you can see works by Albania's most famous painters of the Middle ages. Onufri (Mid 16th century) and David Selenica (early 18th century) as well as beautiful works by anonymous goldsmiths, silversmiths, woodcarvers and armourers. One of its greatest treasures is an 10th century iconostasis carved under the direction of the master Dhimiter.

The National Museum of Education opened in 1967 in the building when the first Albanian school was set up.

The Museum of the National Liberation War.

The district of Korca has picturesque countryside which is worth visiting, regardless of the narrow roads leading to it. The village of Dardha is an ideal spot for winter sports, such as skiing. Another village is Bilishti in the region of Devoll, the road passes through the beautiful valley of the Devoll river.

West of Korca at a distance of 24 kms, is situated the village of Voskopoja, known since the 14th century. during the 17th and 18th centuries Voskopoja has been a flourishing town. During the 18th century, Voskopoja had an Academy and a Printing Press and was a well-known centre of art, where some of the most talented Albanian painters practised their profession. At the 2nd half of the 18th century Voskopoja was ruined and turned again into a village as it had been originally.

The pillaging of the town, especially of its treasures, of the records and manuscripts of its churches continued even during the 1st and 2nd World Wars. Of the many churches of this once prosperous town, built during the 16th-18th centuries, there have remained but a few. Of some interest are the St Nicholaus church, the mural paintings of which were made by the Korca painters, the Kostantin and Athanas brothers and by David from Selenica and the Monastery of St. Prodhan, burned down during the 2nd World War, where some of the exquisite mural paintings are kept intact.

Tourists may spend their nights in Korca at "Llira" hotel. This hotel provides a small local band which plays characteristic songs and dances of the district as well as foreign.

Leaving Korca in the southerly direction of the mountainous region of Kolonja. The road passes through the village of Kamenica, through the Pass of Qarr (Qafe Qarr) and the villages of Qinam-Radovicke, and to the small town of Erseka, which has a population of 5,000 inhabitants.

The road then continues southward, through the villages of Tac and Borova. On the 6th July 1943, the German occupation troops massacred 107 women, old man and children and erased the village to the ground. The event is commemorated by a monument and a museum. The monument is situated on the top of a hill on the right of the road, and is in the form of a spiral. To top circle has 107 stones, symbols of the innocent killed. Nearby are the remains of an Illyrian settlement of the 7th and 2nd century B.C. then the road passes through the gorge of Barmash to the villages of Barmash and Germenj and then to the town of Leskovik near the Greek border. Not far from the village of Leskovik, there is a Spa, which is a popular destination because of its healing qualities.

<u>PERMET</u> : The road then turns north-westward through the villages of Carshova, Pellumbar, Petran to the town of Permet. Permet is a small town, which is mentioned for the first time by this name in documents of the 15th century. Permet was burned down four times during the National Liberation war. Here was held in May 1944 the first Antifascist National Liberation Congress. Permet is now the administrative centre of the district, with a population of 6,000 inhabitants. It is a centre of light and food industries with flour mill, factories for the production of knitwear, woodwork, building materials and pasta, as well as for the processing of grapes. It has a factory producing wine and raki. The wine and raki of Permet (Labelled "Permet") are the best in the country. We suggest for you to buy as a souvenir "Permet" or "Kaberneti" (Berat) wine.

Permet is famous for its beautiful folk songs accompanied by the characteristic instrument, clarinet. If you come across any cassette with Permeti songs, do not miss the opportunity of buying them.

The road then takes you though the village of Kosina to the small town of Kelcyra, which is mentioned in a document of 1272 under the name of Klousura. It dominated the strategic gorge of Kelcyra and in the nearby mount of Trebeshina are the ruins of an Illyrian fortress built in the 4th and 5th centuries B.C. and rebuilt in the pre-Ottoman Middle Ages. The town has a brickwork, a cannery and a factory engaged in grape processing. At the Gorge of Kelcyra (Gryka e Kelcyres) there is a bar providing coffee and drinks.

The itinerary then follows the roads through Tapelena, Gjirokastra, Saranda and the trip back on the coastline of Ionian sea, having lunch at Vlora and ending up in Durres. The following day, you have lunch in Durres and leave through Rinas Airport (refer to Itinerary One for details of these town guides).

# ITINERARY - THREE

## ITINERARY - THREE

| | | |
|---|---|---|
| Hani i Hotit | -Shkodra | 1 (one night) |
| Shkodra | -Tropoja | 2 (two nights) |
| Tropoja | -Kukes | 2 (two nights) |
| Kukes | -Tirana | 1 (one night) |
| Tirana | -Peshkopia | 2 (two nights) |
| Peshkopia | -Durres | 1 (one night) |
| Durres | -Shkodra | 1 (one night) |
| Shkodra | -Hani i Hotit | (departing). |

This is the longest itinerary, which includes the trip to the north and Northeastern regions of Albania. The more you travel into the interiors of the country, the more you learn about Albania's customs and traditions. It is in the mountains that the essential inwardness of Albanian life becomes more apparent.

Tourists can travel from Hani i Hotit and follow the track of the ancient highway, down into the plain of upper Shkodra. To the east lies the mountainous district of Malesia e Madhe (The Greater Highlands). After spending a night in Shkodra, you drive Northeast, towards the region of Tropoja. The road passes through some villages of Shkodra and runs in a series of sharp bends, to the lake of Koman. Koman is the biggest hydropower station in Albania (600,0000 KW/h). At Koman you take the boat to Fierza. This is one of the most impressive voyages through the river Drini. The river, with the high rocky mountains on the background, makes the scenery very attractive. After two hours sailing through the calm waters of the river, you reach Fierza (a village included in Tropoja district), where there is built the second biggest hydropower station in the country, with a capacity of 500,000 KW/h. Having crossed a bridge, you follow the valley of Valbona (Lugina e Valbones), which follows into the Drin just below the dam and comes to the village of Bujan. Bujan is the birthplace of Mic Sokoli, a hero of the League of Prizren, who died gloriously in the battle of Slivova, 1818, hurling himself on the Turkish cannon. The house in which he was born, a very typical, 3-storey-kulla (tower-house) was opened as a museum in 1978.

It was in this village that in December 31, 1943, was held the conference with Albanian and Yugoslav representatives, who decided to unify Kosovo territory with Albania. In the year 1913, at the London Conference, the great powers decided that Kosovo should pass over to Serbia, as a sop, the region becoming a backwater of the emergent Yugoslav state. World War II didn't help Kosovo. In 1945 it still remained part of Serbia within the Socialist Federation of South Slav people. Tito crushed any sign of a nationalist opposition and filled all the region's keyposts with outsiders. The Albanian people were subsequently harried by the UDBA (The Secret Police) and the Serbian Police Force.

In the mid-1960's, Tito and his allies decided to liberalize the regime and reform the UDBA. With the lid off, Kosovo exploded, and 1968 saw serious rioting events which persuaded Tito to rethink his policy and institute a series of reforms designed to give back some measure of autonomy. The population of Kosovo remained very poor, unemployment stayed absurdly high and the gap between Kosovo and richer areas, like Slovania, seemed to be ever-widening. The mid 1980's were a period of repression; Belgrade stepping up efforts to stifle all nationalist opposition in the province, but doing little to solve the underlying problems. As the economic crises in the country deepened, and dissent over solutions grew throughout Yugoslavia, so conditions became ideal for the resurgence of Serb nationalism under the Serbian Party leader, Slobodan Milosovic.

In the spring of 1981, student demonstrations ignited the hitherto, concealed economic and ethnic resentments that had been smouldering away for years. The result was rioting that left 11 people dead and over 200 badly injured. Belgrade reacted forcefully; local government and party officials were purged and the army sealed off the whole area, taking over 1000 activists away to Prison, where some 400 remain serving terms of 15 years or more.

Leaving behind the village of Bujan you drive through the district of Tropoja, (also know as "Malesia e Gjakoves" - "Gjakova Highland") Northeast of Bujan an enclosing well of dressed stone, marks the city of the Illyrian citadel of Rosnje, built in the 4th century B.C. on the frontier between the Lebeates and the Dardanians. Excavation has yielded tools, pottery and coins., which bear witness to fairly considerable activity from the Iron age to the christian age. 8 km away from Bujan is the town of Bajram Curri included in Tropoja district. The town was known as Kolgecaj until 1952, when it was renamed in honour of the great patriot Bajram Curri (1862-1965), who took an active part in the Albanian movement towards freedom and independence. A sworn enemy to Ahmet Zogu, who had him condemned to death in 1922, he was one of the inspirations for the 1924 revolution. In the town's main square is an imposing bronze statue of Bajram Curri.

*What to visit:*

The Local Historical Museum, which reveals the struggle of the Tropoja and Kosovo people for independence and freedom. The traditions and customs of Tropoja are the same as Kosovo people. The majority of Tropoja inhabitants have relatives in Kosovo. This museum displays a large variety of object and materials, witnessing the rich culture and the history of the region.

*VALBONA*: Continuing on the road, you come to Margegaj village, an administrative centre of the Upper Valbona Valley. Not far from Margegaj is situated Shoshan village where there is a picturesque spring (Vrella e Shoshanit), the most abundant in the Northern Alps. The road continues to climb, running alongside the river, whose crystal waters are well-stocked with trout. Through forests of beech and sweet chestnut, mingled increasingly with conifers.

Before reaching Dragobi village, on the leftside flows a channel deriving from Valbona river. This channel is known as the channel of Bajram Curri. Some 15 km away from the town, to the left of the road is the Dragobi Cave (Shpella e

Dragobise), where Bajram Curri was killed.

On the way to Valbona village, you can have some photo-stops, which will help remind you of the beautiful scenery of the Alps in Valbona river. Three km before arriving at Valbona village, (where the hotel is situated), is a beautiful lake which is fed by the springs of Valbona river. After 5 minutes walk through the forest, a bewitching scenery unfolds in front of you. The calm waters of the blue and green coloured lake, reflecting the rich vegetation growing in the surroundings and on the background, the majestic high Alps echoing the birds' songs and the buzzing of the insects. One can not help the feeling of looking down at the waters, staring at your reflection and "not by accident" gazing at the trouts which sometimes swim at the very surface, stirring the tranquillity of the natural mirror in front of you.

You then drive to the village of Valbona, situated at the entrance to an imposing cirque surrounded by bare and jagged mountains rising to over 2500 metres. There is a striking contrast between the pyramid-shaped mountains and the deep valleys between them which have the form of narrow gorges on deep hollows. To the left, is the group of mountain known as "Grykat e Hepeta" (The Great Gorges), the highest peak of which is 2525 metres; to the right is "Mali i Kollates" (Kollata Mountain) (2555 metres) and straight ahead is mountain Jezerca, the highest peak in Northern Albania (2694 metres)

Another picturesque spot is "Fusha e Gjehve" (Cattle Plain). This plain is surrounded by high mountains on all sides. It is an excellent place for picnic. You may have a packed lunch here enjoying the scenery and the fresh mountain air. At winter time, this area is covered by snow. North has a very healthy climate, and the Albanian mountaineers are strong, tall and live longer than the rest of the Albanian population.

You can spend a night at Valbona Hotel, which is provided with the necessary facilities. Next day you drive back to the town of Tropoja where you spend the night at "Shkelzeni" or "Kosovo" hotel.

*TROPOJA* : is famous for chestnuts. It has the biggest plantations in the country. Here grow, figs, apples and plums, which are of good quality. This region is rich in mineral resources, especially in chromium and boxides, copper, kaolin and magnetite deposits.

Having spend two nights in Tropoja, you depart early in the morning and take a ferry back to Koman. At Koman you take a drive to Kukes. On the way to Kukes, you pass the village of Qerret, and see the ruins of the Medieval fortress of Dalmacia.

Then you enter the small town of Puka. This is the town, where a great poet, Migjeni worked. The region of Puka has 50,000 inhabitants. Puka is among the districts which ranks highest in the field of wood-working. The main branch of industry is the mining and the enrichment of copper. The mountainous district of Puka is rich in forest. Here are situated the biggest saw mills in the country. Having a coffee stop in Puka, you drive to Fushe Arrez (which is an industrial town included in Puka district) famous for the processing of timber and up-grading of copper.

From Fushe Arrez, after some km, you are at the summit of "Qafe e Malit" (Mountain Pass). Having passed the villages of Shemri and Kolsh, you emerge into the new town of Kukes.

*KUKES* : The full name of Kukes is Kikesi i Ri (New Kukes). The original town was engulfed in 1976, by the waters of the large artificial lake (area 72.5 km) formed to supply the Fierza Hydropower station. The town of Kukes has a population of 12000 inhabitants.

Kukes is completely new, built during the 70's. The old town of Kukes is submerged under the waters.

This district is mainly mountainous. The highest peak is that of Gjalica (2480m). The mountains are covered by industrially important forests, the geological structure of the area has determined the existence of innumerable ores such as coper and chromium. The Highlanders in the region, are well known for their developed agriculture.

Kukes has a carpet factory whose products are for domestic and trade use. There is also a copper processing factory as the raw material, copper, is found in this place.

You can spend two nights at the new hotel of Kukes, which overlooks the artificial lake, provided with all the necessary facilities. This hotel is one of the best in Albania.

The following day you have the chance to explore the beauties of the lake, sailing through its calm waters. The delicious lunch served on the boat and the swimming is the highlight of the trip.

*What to visit :*

The Local Historical Museum and Carpet Factory.

The houses of Kukes, as well as other northern regions of Albania have a unique architecture, which can not be found in other parts of the country. These huge, stony houses, known as "Kulla", look like fortresses in miniature. What strikes one's eyes are the small wooden windows (known as - frengji), guarding through the thick walls the surrounding area from the enemies. "Kullas" have been subject to discussions by many historians. There were hypothesis that "kullas" with their fortress - like shape, served as protection from the bloodfeud; but the very cannon of Lek Dukagjini (the lawyer of bloodfeud), refutes this idea:

"The revenger has no right to fire on women, children, cattle and houses..."

Shtjefen Gjecovi Kryeziu (1933)
(Cannon of Lek Dukagjini)

So, it is reasonable that the "Kullas" were there to protect the family from any attack by invaders.

The law of Lek covers inheritance and crime, especially murder, bodily assault and theft (1444- 1489).

Lek Dukagjin, lord of Dagno and Zadrima, who fled with others to Italy in 1479 when the Turks captured Shkoder, returned after the death of Sultan Mehmet II in 1481, and prescribed and enforced punishment for crime in the Northern Albanian Highlands. Crime was checked by the prescription of specific punishments and enforced by a Council of Tribal Elders Vendetta (called like this from Sicily) because a blood-feud could quickly have degenerated into mass extermination without a code of honour to which all males had to subscribe (there was no blood feud affecting women protected either alone or escorted by men-folk, as well as children, cattle, house). Albanian's have a peculiar sensitivity to a perceived affront, whether by physical blow, verbal insult, or even dispute on a matter of fact. The intrusion of the family honour demanded a blood feud on the part of the eldest male of the family, who would kill the person responsible for this. Killing was not punishable for adultery or rape, or if a murderer was sought out and killed the same day. Wounding was merely fined according to the degree of injury. And so revenge, this contagious disease was transmitted from generation to generation, leaving behind tracks filled with blood, guiding aimlessly through a dark life. After a couple of mutual killings, the reason vanished and there was only the duty to perform.

-The houses were full of rifles! - writes the English traveller, Edith Durham, in her book "High Albania" (1909) "Vraka (a village in the North). It is made up of various families that had fled, because they owed blood, from Bosnia and Montenegro about 200 years ago. The men could not leave the village for fear of being shot by Muslims, so it was left to the women to travel to Scutari to do the business of the bazaar". Durham, this civilized lady, repeatedly inquired about blood feuds at each village she visited.

Boga - seventy five families, all Catholic, unlike its brethren Vulki and Seltze, was rife with bloodfeuds. Two brothers had recently been shot by their own relative" - she wrote.

Sometimes, the murderer could ask the council for a besa, or truce. If granted, elders were appointed by the murderer and the Lord of Blood (Zot i Gjakut) of the Council of elders, to explore the possibilities of a just settlement, and ensure that it was sworn in the local church or mosque. A permanent besa between families or tribes was effected by a marriage alliance.

"As the bereaved and the killer's family come to an agreement to forgive the crime, they decide to drink from each other's blood!" Shtjefen Gjecovi, Cannon of Lek Dukagjini.

Blood feud does not exist any more in Albania. It vanished through years. In a discussion we had with an old mountaineer from Dukagjini, he told us that the last killing was in 1918. After that no one was killed!". Any attempt for murder or intended crime is now punished according to the state law.

You leave Kukes early in the morning and drive toward Tirana. On the Way to Tirana you stop at the Hunting Lodge of Lezha and visit the town of Kruja.

Having spent a night in Tirana, you leave for Peshkopia, a mountainous town situated in the Northeast of Albania. The road continues through mixed beech and coniferous forest to Burrel, to the chief town of the Mat region, Burrel. It has a population of 8,000 inhabitants. Burrel has a plant for the treatment of chromium ore, set up in 1979. In this area the old regional costumes can still be seen in every day use - though now increasingly confined to the wearing of the traditional qeleshe (felt cap) by men and scarf covering their head with a point hanging low down on the back, by women.

Burrel is the birthplace of Pjeter Budi (1566 - 1622), bishop of Sada (Naoshurdah) who is noted for his literary works and who was also a member of the group who tried to persuade the Pope to organize a crusade for the liberation of Albania.

Mustafa Xhani (1910 - 1947) called Baba Faja, Chief Father of the Teqe of Martanesh made it a centre of Anti-fascist resistance.

Mat is known for mining and the ferro-chromium metallurgy. The district has a large food processing and timber industry. The district has two hydropower stations, which have been set up on the Mati river. Sheep and goats are raised on the hilly and mountainous areas.

The road then leaves the Mat valley and begins to climb, passing a mountainous road through a series of villages. There are fine views on the left and then on the right. On the right, one can see a typical old house of the Mat region with a Tyrbe and a kulla (fortified tower). Much altered, but still recognizable and still inhabited. The road continues to ascend with beautiful views to the Qarri Pass and then descends by

way of Bulqiza, with a factory on the right. Bulqiza is a new miners town. Mineral ores, such as chrome, marble and sulphur have been discovered in this area. It is the biggest chrome centre in Albania and one of the biggest in Europe.

Some 30 minutes drive from Bulqiza is situated the picturesque village of Zerqan. Once, driving to Peshkopia, we came across a group of people on horses riding in a line. The horses in front were beautifully decorated with multi-coloured scarfs and flowers and on its back was riding a woman who had covered her face with a red veil. The tourists became curious and decided to stop the bus and enquire about these people. Soon, we learned that the horse riders were wedding hosts, and the woman in the front was the bride. It was very impressive for the tourists who started to take pictures of the caravan. The bride's father invited us all to the wedding. We ended up at the wedding party riding horses, which were kindly offered to us by the wedding hosts. It was a wonderful wedding. The tourists danced Albanian folk dances and sang songs. All sang, joining the 80 other participants. Next morning the master of the house gave a large bottle of raki to the tourists and bid us a nice trip to Peshkopia.

In return, for the pleasant evening, the tourists gave small presents to the newly married couple.

A few villages in Albania still preserve old customs and traditions in weddings. Marriages used to be arranged by matchmakers. A young woman could be married off to an old man for the interest of the clan or for money. Women suffered from the discrimination determined by the feudal moral norms and backward customs. The birth of a girl was considered a misfortune and a burden on the family. Parents sometimes named the girl "Sose" which meant "Ending", so that there would not be any other girl in the family. In certain regions the woman were compelled to cover her face with yashmak. Frequently men referred to women as "long-haired, but short-minded creatures". Under these conditions the participation of women in state employment was something quite extraordinary. Women did all house work and field work. A well known Albanian writer Cajupi used to write "Men in the shadow play and talk, damned them, they live at women's expense".

Time was needed to change the woman's position in society. At present you don't find women wearing yashmak and there is a large number of women working in all walks of life. But still we cannot say that women are fully emancipated. The old mentality is deeply rooted and it is very difficult to do away with it. A clear example of such a mentality are the fully crowded bars and clubs in most of the towns (even in the Capital), with men and if by chance a woman enters, she will have to face hundreds of eyes staring at her in surprise. Many women tourists have faced such a problem and have been surprised that "even in the 20th century in this part of Europe, women are still inferior to men". In spite of the mentality inherited from the past 50 years long communist regime, praised the emancipation of women only in one direction: state work, but too little or nothing was done as far as her spiritual problems are concerned. Communism in Albania put women in a cage, so that she suffered a double isolation : in society and family terms.

Love relations to a boy, without being married to him, was considered as "immoral", "capitalistic, "bourgeois", and many other epithets of the kind. Hence, the backward mentality inherited from the past was trimmed by the State-Party into a "moderated fanaticism"

Nowadays marriages are mainly based on love. When the boy and the girl come to an agreement, both families (bride's and bridegroom's) decide upon the date of the marriage. The new couple go through the official marriage ceremony in an authorized office, where at the presence of a witness, they exchange rings. Now, the new couple can organize the wedding ceremony in church.

Wedding parties are very big; sometimes with the participation of 100-150 guests. They take place on Saturday evening (for the bride's family) and on Sunday evening (for the bridegroom's family). The wedding dinner is very rich; people are offered several drinks and dishes and there is a band playing all night long.

Until this year Albanian couples had to rely on traditional methods of family planning to regulate their fertility. Both modern contraception and legal abortion were available only on medical grounds. Within the framework of the general democratization, the government had adopted a new family planning policy, which is in accordance with the methods and practices of MNFPA.

We now continue our trip toward the last town in the visit list; Peshkopia.

The road runs along side the Mati river for a time, then crosses it and comes to the Diber road on the right, shortly before Maqullara. After a road on the right to Herbel, which has an interesting church, the main road continues through apple orchards, passes the village of Melan and comes to Peshkopia.

*PESHKOPIA* : lies on the eastern part of Albania, on either side of the Black Drini river. The Drini valley is the lowest part of the district. The Korabi peak (2751 m) is the country's highest peak, which is situated in this district. Peshkopia has a population of 10,000 inhabitants.

Mineral ores such as chromium, sulphur, marble have been discovered in this district. The thermal mineral water springs are situated in the vicinity of Peshkopia and have important medicinal values.

*What to visit:*

The Ethnographic Museum, situated in a characteristic dwelling house. Here you will be introduced to an excellent collection of local costumes, carpets, kitchen equipment and filigree jewellery, as well as a number of models of local architecture.

Lura with its 7 glacial lakes are famous for their natural beauty. Lura mountain climbs up to a height 1600 - 1700 m with magnificent beech trees and higher up conifers. The highest point, a bare peak called "Kurora e Lures" (Lura's Crown) rises to 2112m, but most visitors will prefer to confine themselves to visiting the lakes which occupy glacial cirques at heights of between 1200 - 1500 m or at best the four principle lakes, the "Leqeni i Madh" (Great Lake), "Leqeni i zi" (Black Lake), "Leqeni i luleve" (Lake of Flowers), and "Liqeni i Lopeve"(Cows' Lake). A full day is required for this visit, as the road is not asphalted and time is needed to explore the beauties of nature this area offers you.

In Peshkopia you can find accommodation at "korabi" hotel. Spending two nights in Peshkopia, you drive back to Durres to spend the last night in Albania.

*So, dear readers, we have guided you along the recess of this "unknown land", called Albania. We have climbed with you rocky mountains, we crossed lovely valleys, driven snaking roads, ridden horses and met local people. Socialism proved to be a disaster in Albania. A system which secured its existence through lies. There is a joke related to it which has recently come out :*

*"Two people living in Paradise were watching through a hole in the ground, to Hell. To their surprise they noticed that people were happy there, dancing, singing and drinking all night long. - Why don't we try to go there? - they asked each other. And so they did. But it turned out that instead of entertainment, a huge devil got them by pitchfork and sent them on fire - No, no - cried the poor man - don't burn us!" - Well, you know this is Hell, and you came here yourselves!, shouted the devil. But, there was entertainment every night here?! - Ha, ha, ha - laughed the devil - its the propaganda section, you fools!"*

TIRANA BUSINESS DIGEST

# TIRANA

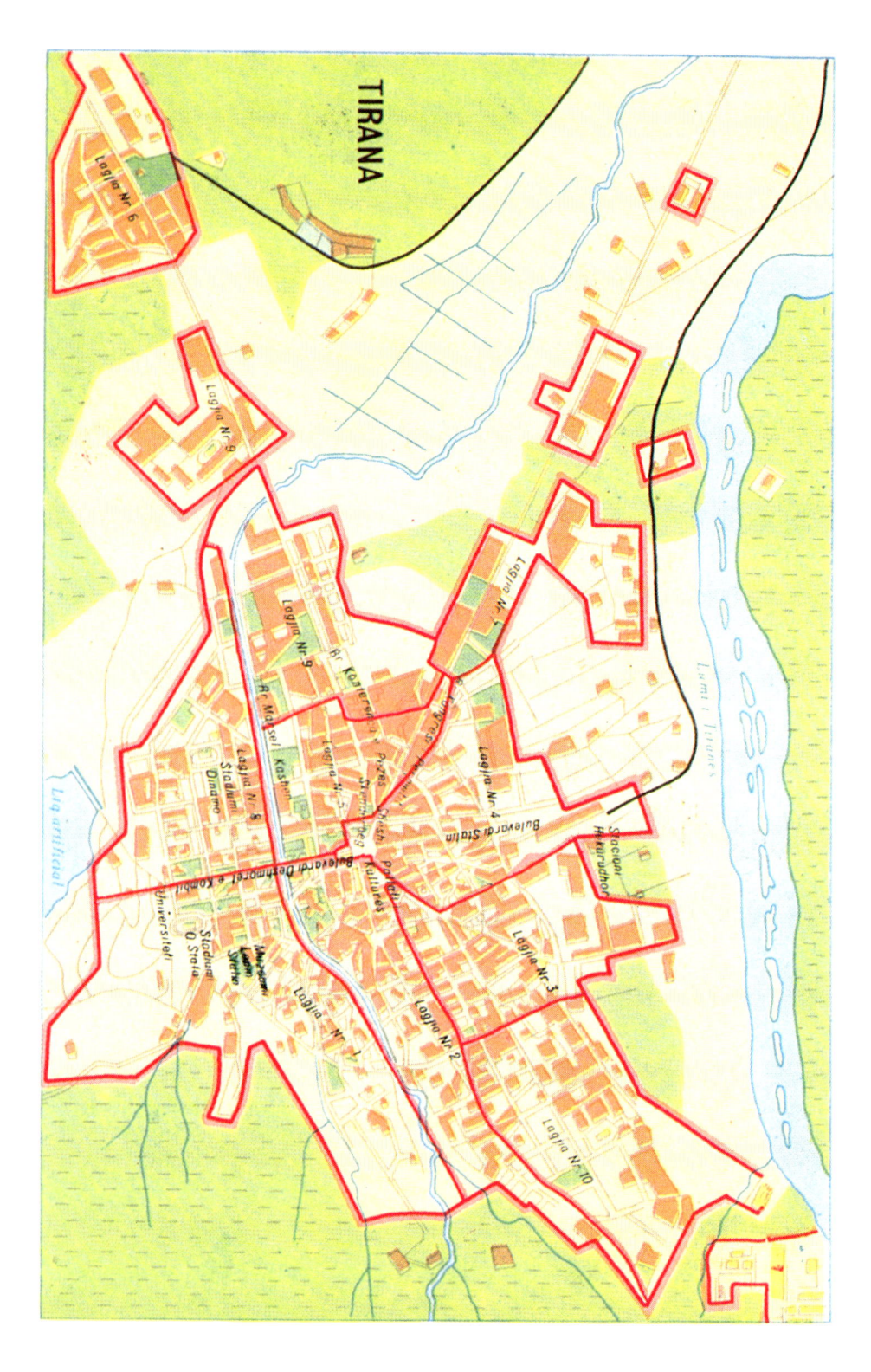

**Contents**

- Embassies.

- Agencies & Ministries.

- Hotels & Restaurants.

- Travel Information.

*Foreign Embassy's.*

* The country code for Albania is 355.
* The area code for Tirana is 42

| Country | Telephone No. |
| --- | --- |
| Algeria | 329-64 |
| Bulgaria | 329-06, 331-55 |
| Czechoslovakia | 321-12 |
| Egypt | 330-22 |
| France | 342-50, 340-54 |
| Greece | 242-90, 342-91 |
| Germany | 320-50, 320-48 |
| Hungary | 322-42, 322-38 |
| Italy | 343-43, 340-14 |
| Yugoslavia | 320-83, 320-91 |
| China | 323-85 |
| Korea | 336-71, 335-73 |
| Cuba | 322-79, 322-82 |
| Libya | 341-06, 340-86 |
| Palestine | 343-00 |
| Poland | 341-90, 335-69 |
| Romania | 322-87 |
| Russia | 345-00 |
| Turkey | 333-94 |
| United Kingdom | 342-50 |
| United States of America | 328-74 |
| Vatican | 335-46 |
| Vietnam | 323-28 |

# ACO UK

The *ACO UK* is a private company, based in England, that specialises in assisting western companies to develop trade and commerce in Albania. Our services include;

- *The identification of specific joint venture opportunities with existing Albanian companies.*

- *The identification and selection of appropriate joint venture partners for new projects.*

- *Consultancy services and trade visits.*

- *Market Research and market identification.*

- *Sourcing manufacturing requirements.*

- *Identifying sources of product for export from Albania.*

So whether you are looking to sell your products directly, find a distributer, set up a sales office, establish a joint venture or set up a new factory, call the experts at;

*ACO UK*
38 Brooke Road
Princes Risborough
Aylesbury
Bucks HP27 9HJ
ENGLAND

Telephone : 44 (0)844 274899

Facsimile : 44 (0)844 274796

*Agencies based in Tirana.*

| | |
|---|---|
| European Community | 283-20, 284-78 |
| UNICEF | 331-22, 331-48 |
| Red Cross | 337-94 |
| World Bank | 286-57 |
| UNDP | 331-22 |
| The Helsinki Albanian Committee | 336-71 |
| Albanian Telegraphic Agency | 341-84 |
| The Institute of Insurance | 238-38 |
| Albanian Chamber of Commerce | 279-97 |
| ALBTURIST Travel Agency | 343-59 |

*Government Ministries in Tirana.*

| | |
|---|---|
| Ministry of Trade | 246-73 |
| Ministry of Finance | 260-01 |
| Ministry of Tourism | 279-31 |
| Ministry of Agriculture | 279-20 |
| Ministry of Health | 264-20 |
| Ministry of Labour | 250-51 |
| Ministry of Construction | 283-07 |
| Ministry of Transport | 268-51 |
| Ministry of Education | 283-04 |
| Ministry of Justice | 283-78 |
| Ministry of Culture | 285-12 |

*Hotels & Restaurants.*

| | |
|---|---|
| Hotel Tirana<br>"Sheshi Skenderbej", Tirana. | 344-47 |
| Hotel Dajti<br>Rr. "Shetitorja Deshmoret e Kombit", Tirana. | 321-72<br>333-26 |
| Rrugova Restaurant<br>Rr. "Konference e Pezes", Tirana. | |
| Berlin Restaurant (see page 109)<br>Rr. "Vaso Pasha" No.7, Tirana. | 333-37 |
| Tirana Restaurant<br>Rr. "Kongresi i Permetit", Tirana. | 266-21 |
| Pelikan Restaurant<br>Rr. "Cerciz Topulli", Tirana. | |
| L'aigle Noir Restaurant<br>24 Rr. "Vildan Luarasi", Tirana. | |
| Ghez Laurent Restaurant<br>Rr. "Konferenca e Pezes" No.17, Tirana. | |

*Private Accommodation Rental.*

| | |
|---|---|
| Tirana Real Estate Agency<br>Teatri i Operas dhe Baletit Tirana. | 331-18 |

*Taxi's.*

Taxi's can be found outside the Dajti and Tirana hotels at most times of the day. To call for a taxi, telephone Albtransport on (42) 230-26.

*Electric Current.*

The system used in Albania is based on the continental European system of 220 volts, using the round two pin plug. A standard European universal adaptor will be adequate.

*Telephone System.*

There are no public telephones available in Tirana. To make an international call from Tirana, it is necessary to use either the Hotel Dajti or Hotel Tirana telephone offices, which also have facsimile facilities. To make international calls from a private telephone it is necessary to dial the operator to book the call. They will ask for the telephone number you wish to call and the number you are dialling from. When they have an international connection they will call you back. This can take upto three hours to achieve.

*Photography and Video Cameras.*

Photographs and the use of video cameras are fully permitted throughout Albania, except for military areas. You will however, need to take all additional film and video cassettes with you, as these are not readily available for sale in Albania.

*Currency and payment for goods.*

The Albanian Lek is now a fully floating currency and is therefore subject to the fluctuations of market forces. Exchange rates are published daily and made available at the State Bank, Dajti and Tirana hotels. American Express is welcomed at most Albturist Hotels, however, neither Visa or Mastercard are accepted. Travellers Cheques and US Dollars can be changed at all hotels and state banks.

All hotels, taxi's and retail outlets are now charging local currency. So it is important to change any foreign currency before attempting to buy goods or services.

*Air Travel.*

Rhinas Airport is Albania's only commercial airport (Albtransport 42 268-90). The following airlines fly to and from this airport;

Alitalia
SwissAir
ADA Air (French-Albanian)
Olympic Airlines (Greek)
Arberia (US-Albanian)
Hemus Air (Bulgarian)
Adria Airways (Slovenian)
Malev Air (Hungarian)
Albanian Airlines (Austrian-Albanian)


*Travel Agency.*

Ilir & Susan Xhelo, Directors
Albanian Travel & Tours
Kongresi i Permetit P.102
Tirana
Albania

Telephone No. 329-83
Facsimile No. 339-81
Telex          2281

Services; Air Tickets, Hotel Reservations, Ferry Tickets (Durres, Saranda, Vlora), Special Group Tours, Hunting Tours, Taxi Service and Private House rental.


Sadik Malaj, President
"Sondor" Travel Agency
Rr. "Alqi Kondi" No.9
Tirana
Albania

Tel/Fax No.    278-57

# REGENT
## HOLIDAYS U.K. LTD.

EXPERT IN TRAVEL TO ALBANIA SINCE 1970

GROUP TOURS &
INDIVIDUAL ARRANGEMENTS

**SPECIAL FARES TO TIRANA AVAILABLE**

**FROM LONDON AND MANCHESTER**

EXPERIENCED AND KNOWLEDGEABLE STAFF

REGENT HOLIDAYS, 15 JOHN STREET,
BRISTOL BS1 2HR, ENGLAND

TEL 0272 211711 (24 hours) FAX 0272 254866

ABTA 51534    IATA    ATOL 856

# ADRIA
## ADRIA AIRWAYS

### FLIGHTS TO TIRANA AVAILABLE FROM LONDON HEATHROW AND MANCHESTER

Adria Airways, established in 1961, became the national airline of Slovenia, following its recent independence. Today Adria flies to 17 destinations in 10 European countries.

**LJUBLJANA:** *Kuzmiceva 7, Ljubljana, Slovenia.*
*Tel; (061) 313366, Fax; (061) 323356*

**NEW YORK:** *Louis Overseas Travel Co Inc, 2325 Arthur Avenue, Bronx, New York 10458 USA. Tel; 212 733 6900, Fax; 212 733 7015*

**LONDON:** *49 Conduit Street, London W1 9FB, United Kingdom.*
*Tel; 44 (071) 734 4630, Fax; 44 (071) 287 5476*

**TIRANA:** *Rruga Kongresi i Permetit pal.102, Tirana, Albania.*
*Tel; 355 (42) 28483, Fax; 355 (42) 28483*

---

First RENT A CAR service in

## ALBANIA

Kompas HERTZ branch office at

## TIRANA AIRPORT

offers a choice of selected fine cars:

- *self drive or chauffeur driven*
- *delivery & collection, 24 hours service*

ALL INFORMATION & RESERVATIONS ARE AVAILABLE THROUGH HERTZ INTERNATIONAL RESEVRATION SYSTEM:

| | | |
|---|---|---|
| U.K., | Tel 44 81 679 1799 | |
| | Fax 44 81 679 0181 | **KOMPAS** |
| USA, | Tel 1 405 755 4400 | |
| | Fax 1 405 728 6300 | **Hertz** |
| Slovenia, | Tel 38 61 572 005 | |
| | Fax 38 61 151 311 | |

## AIRLINE SCHEDULE FOR TIRANA AIRPORT

### April 1993 - March 1994

| Day | Carrier | Destination | Arrive | Depart |
|---|---|---|---|---|
| MONDAY | Albanian Airlines | Munich | 16:55 | 10:10 |
| | ADA AIR | Bari | 14:30 | 10:10 |
| | Albanian Airlines | Vienna | 13:30 | 13:55 |
| | Alitalia | Rome | 12:45 | 13:25 |
| | SwissAir | Zurich | 15:15 | 16:10 |
| | MALEV | Budapest | 16:10 | 16:55 |
| | Albanian Airlines | Rome | 21:55 | 17:25 |
| | ADA AIR | Bari | - | 18:30 |
| TUESDAY | Albanian Airlines | Zurich | 16:05 | 08:05 |
| | ADA AIR | Bari | 09:45 | 10:10 |
| | Olympic | Athens | 11:45 | 12:25 |
| | Alitalia | Rome | 12:40 | 13:25 |
| | Albanian Airlines | Vienna | 13:30 | 13:55 |
| | Hemus Air | Sofia | 13:00 | 14:00 |
| | ADA AIR | Bari | 14:30 | 18:30 |
| | Adria Air | Ljubljana | 21:50 | - |
| WEDNESDAY | Adria Air | Ljubljana | - | 06:50 |
| | ADA AIR | Bari | 09:05 | 10:10 |
| | Albanian Airlines | Munich | 16:55 | 10:10 |
| | Alitalia | Rome | 12:45 | 13:25 |
| | Albanian Airlines | Vienna | 13:30 | 13:55 |
| | SwissAir | Zurich | 15:15 | 16:10 |
| | Albanian Airlines | Rome | 21:55 | 17:25 |
| | ADA AIR | Bari | 14:30 | 18:30 |
| | Adria Air | Ljubljana | 21:50 | - |

| | | | | |
|---|---|---|---|---|
| THURSDAY | Adria Air | Ljubljana | - | 06:50 |
| | Albanian Airlines | Zurich | 10:05 | 08:05 |
| | ADA AIR | Bari | 09:05 | 10:10 |
| | Olympic | Athens | 12:00 | 12:40 |
| | Alitalia | Rome | 12:45 | 13:25 |
| | MALEV | Budapest | 13:35 | 14:20 |
| | ADA AIR | Bari | 14:30 | 18:30 |
| FRIDAY | MALEV | Budapest | 08:35 | 09:20 |
| | ADA AIR | Bari | 09:05 | 10:10 |
| | Albanian Airlines | Munich | 16:55 | 10:10 |
| | Alitalia | Rome | 12:45 | 13:25 |
| | Albanian Airlines | Vienna | 13:30 | 13:55 |
| | SwissAir | Zurich | 15:15 | 16:10 |
| | ADA AIR | Bari | 14:30 | 18:30 |
| SATURDAY | ADA AIR | Bari | 12:30 | 09:00 |
| | Albanian Airlines | Rome | 14:15 | 09:20 |
| | Alitalia | Rome | 12:40 | 13:25 |
| | Adria Air | Ljubljana | 21:50 | - |
| SUNDAY | Adria Air | Ljubljana | - | 06:50 |
| | ADA AIR | Bari | 15:30 | 12:00 |
| | Alitalia | Rome | 12:45 | 13:25 |
| | Hemus Air | Sofia | 13:00 | 14:00 |

In addition Arberia Airlines operate scheduled flights New York - Tirana -New York and ICPI Airlines operate scheduled flights Tirana - Istanbul - Tirana.

*Visas.*

European Community and United States citizens do not need visas prior to visiting Albania. An entry tax is payable at the passport control desk in the Airport and at border crossings.

**BULGARIAN AVIATION COMPANY**

# HEMUS AiR Ltd

*the ideal partner for everyone*

*who wishes to save time*

REGULAR, CHARTER AND CARGO FLIGHTS

Hemus Air Ltd, Sofia Airport, Bulgaria
Telephone; 72-07-54, Facsimile; 79-63-80

Rruga "Kongresi i Permetit"
P.164, Tirana, Albania

---

# ACO UK

## Business Travellers

To ensure that your business trip to Albania is a success, why not let the experts organise the complete package;

- Flights
- Hotel Accommodation
- Interpreter
- Motor Car
- Scheduled meetings with Ministry's
- Meetings with Joint Venture partners
- Factory and site visits

ACO UK, 38 Brooke Road, Princes Risborough, Aylesbury, Bucks HP27 9HJ, ENGLAND
Tel: 44 (0)844 274899      Fax : 44 (0)844 274796

# BIBLIOGRAPHY

Albanian Life (Journal of the Albanian Society) 3.90/1/91

Albanian Life (Journal of the Albanian Society) No. 1. 1989

Arben Pluto, Stefanaq Pollo, "Histoire de l'Albanie des orgines a nois jours" (History of Albania from the Origin to the Present Days)

Besnick Mustafaj, "Entre crime et Mirage de l'albanie" (Vacant Pedestals) 1991.

Edith Durham, "High Albania"

E. Hoxha, Works, Volume 53, 1976

Fan. S. Noli, Works, Volume 3, 1987

Ismail Kadare, Autobiografi e Pipullit tim ne Vargje (The Autobiography of the Albanian People in verse).

Migjeni, Vepra Letrare, Botim i Kosoves (Literary Works. Kosova Edition)

Nagel's Encyclopedia - Guide Albania, 1977

Neritan Ceka, Apollonia 1985

Steven Runciman, Edward Lear - Journals of a Landscape Painter in Greece and Albania, 1988

Shtjefen Gjecovi Kryeziu, Kanuni i Lek Dukagjinit (lek Dukagjini Code), 1933

Tourist Guide Book of Albania. 1969. "Naim Frasheri" Publishing House

Thomas Blagg, an Archaeological and Historical Tour of Albania, 1989

William B. Bland, A short Guide to Albania, 1987.

# LITERATURE

"History has shown that if actions speak louder than words, literature often speaks louder than actions. (I.K.0) The earliest written document which is known dates only from 1462. The first book in Albanian, written by a priest named Gjon Buzuku ; "The Missal" was published in 1555. This liturgy in Geg, the northern dialect of Albania "The Missal". ("Meshari") is mainly of linguistic interest, in particular it shows that at the period, the northern and southern dialects were less differentiated than they later became.

There is another work of the 16th century written also by a priest, Luk Matremga, a member of a family from Himara, which had settled in Palermo, published in Rome in 1592 under the title (E Mesuame e Echraesterae), "Christian Doctrines", this is a translation into the southern dialect, Tosk.

From the 17th century, we have a number of religious books by Pjeter Buli (1566-1689) and others. The literature of 18th century is of very different character. Geg writing now disappears almost completely. The only name to note is that of Jul Zariboba (1724-1788) whose collection of poems "Ghiella es Muriis Virghina" (Life of the Vergime, Marry") was printed in Rome in 1972. Most of the writers of this period were Albanian Moslems using the Tosk dialect, but writing in Arabic characters.

The National Renaissance of the 19th century produced a flowering of secular, romantic literature typified by the poem "Milosao's Songs" (1836) (Kenget e Milosaos) by Jeronim de Rada (1814 - 1903), but the writer who dominated the Albanian literature at this period was the poet Naim Frasheri (1846-1900), author of the pastoral poem "Flocks and Farming" (Bageti e Bujqesi) (1886) and the collection of poems "Summer Flowers" (Lulet e Veres). His (Parajsa dhe Fjala Fluturakc) "Paradise and fugitive Words" and the long epic poem (Histori e Skenderbeut) "History of Scanderbeg" are primarily historic works. Also of importance are his love poems (Bukuri) "Beauty"; his religious poems (Qerbela) and his philosophical poems (Prendia) "The Eternal". Naim's brother, Sami Frasheri (1850-1904) wrote (Shqiperia, c'ka qene, c'eshte dhe c'do te behet) "Albania, what it was, what it is and what it will be" (1899) which became the manifesto of the national movement. Other notable names of Renaissance are : Ndre Mjeda (1866-1937), a catholic priest from Shkodra and Andon Zako Cajupi (1866-1930); his collection of poems "Old Father Tomorr" (Baba Tomorri) published in 1902. Other writers are Luigj Filip Shkodra and Asdreni.

The Albanian's who lived in Italy (the Arberesh) did not remain inactive such as Jeronim De Rada (1814-1903) - his most important work being (Skenderbeu i Pafat) "The Unfortunate Scanderbeg", an epic in 12 books. Many of those writers wrote in other languages, such as Naim Frasheri wrote in Greek, Sami Frasheri in Turkish, Zef Serembe in Italian, Pashko Vasa in Italian and French. The period following Independence in 1912, was dominated by Fan Stilian Noli (1882-1965), who translated many world masterpieces into Albanian and was the author of "The History of Scanderbeg" (Historia e Skenderbeut), "the Dragobi Cave" (Shpella e Dragobise), "Death of an Outlaw" (Syrgjyn Vdekur), etc. His translations of Cervantes, Edgar Allan Poe, Ibsen, Omar Khayyam and above all, Shakespeare, are accepted as models of their kind.

The culmination of the realistic trend was reached in the work of Millosh Gjergj Nikolla (Migjeni, 1911-1938), who wrote both poems and short-stories. He died of tuberculosis at the age of 27. His work was brought together in a number of collections: "Songs of Resurrection" (Kanget e Ringjalljes); "Songs of Affliction" (Kanget e Mjerimit); "Songs of Youth (Kanget e Rinise) etc. Migjeni is otherwise known as the poet of the misery. His poems and short-stories give a clear picture of life under misery:

"The eve and the heart are saddened
at the hour of death, when veins fall silent
to the highest heavens soars the grave
with a desperate scream of suffering and pain.."

"Autumn in nature and autumn in our faces
weep, desires, children of life's misery
weep and lament over the corpses
which autumn adorns with her withered branches"

(Autumn on Parade).

Another outstanding author of this time is Gjergj Fishta, an ex-catholic priest. His book of poems (Lahuta e Malesise) "Mountain Lahuta", is unique for its patriotic spirit and great affection for his motherland - Albania.

After liberation (1944), the dominant literary trend became that of socialist realist. All literary works used to be checked by special commission at the Central Committee of the Party of Labor. Being nailed within the rigid framework of the mon-party ideology, nearly all the literary works lacked originality, inspiration, freedom and not rarely were dried out of artistic quality resulting into mere "political" and "ideological" reading materials. Literary translations consisted of such socialist writers as: Gorki, Tolstoi, London, Dickens, etc. Consequently, Albanian's had a mangled knowledge on the World literature. There were lots of distinguished writers left in oblivion because of their "capitalist" and "revisionist" outlook. The people were served ready-made artistic books, avoiding any self-selection; it was like collectivizing all the people into a large state-property. The results were "excellent" - collective minds, supervised by a "supreme brain" and this is the essence of the socialist realism. The mechanism of such a system is given in the well known novel "Vacant Pedestals" written by Besnik Mustafaj, the Chief Editor of the "World Literature" magazine:

"The life under dictatorship makes history oldish, and similarly mystifies it, deprives the individual from "the self-belief" of influencing ever so little in changing the course of life; especially under the proletarian dictatorship when by all means, continuously and persistently is preached the weakness of the individual and the "magic power" of collectivity."

In spite of that, there are some writers who have made a

number of valuable literary works. To be mentioned is Albania's most prominent intellectual, Ismail Kadare. On the purely literary level, he has often been compared to Gabriel Garcia Marquez, the slot generally reserved for historically rooted ironists and exotic story-tellers with a streak of the fantastic. Kadare is above all a tale-singer. His first novel, "The General of the Dead Army" (1970), which was translated into more than a dozen languages, single handedly putting Albanian literature on the world map (and on the screen, in a French-Italian co-production, starring Marcello Mastroyanni and Michael Piccoli). The story of an Italian general who return to Albania after World War II to collect the remains of his fallen compatriots, is a remarkable meditation, both great and ironic, in the relationship between a country and its former occupier

Other works written by Ismail Kadare are "Drums of the Rain and "The Great Winter" (1972), "Chronicle in Stone" (1973); Kadare's most beautifully written novel is an autobiographical work about his wartime childhood in the Southern Albanian town of Gjirokastra. In a number of novels Kadre finds inspiration in the native legends and historical event. "Twilight of the Gods of the Steppe" (1980), "The Nook of Shame" (1984), "Who Killed Doruntina" (1986) etc., are some of the novels of this kind. The latter novel is set in a Medieval Albanian town. The young woman of the title marries into a family from a distant country, and her brother constantine give his (Besa), or sworn word to his mother that he will being her back whenever she is needed. Constantine is killed in battle, but when the grieving mother, curses her son for not keeping the (Besa), Doruntina, shows up on her mother's doorstep, a few weeks later claiming that was indeed her brother who had brought her back. Out of this simple legend, Kadare fashions a metaphysical detective story, an investigation into the power of a homegrown legend like the Besa to transcend adversity-be it death, foreign occupation or, by modern extension the invasion of a foreign ideology by the state - and define the national identity of people.

"Broken April" which was made into an excellent movie, describes the machinery of vengeance, this social infection, borrowed from one generation to the other.

Ismail Kadare defected to France in 1991 where he still lives with his family. His defection was announced on October 25, followed by a declaration to "Le Monde" that the "promises of democratization are dead".

Another outstanding write is Dritero Agolli (1931) with his novels "Greatness and Decline of Comrade Zylo", "The Man with Cannon", "Commander Memo" etc which are quite popular. He is the author of some poems "Mother Albania", "Poems for my father and for me" etc.

Other writers to be mentioned are Kol Jakova, Llazar Siliqi, Teodor Laco, Lasgush Poradeci, Dhimiter Shuteriqi, Fatmir Gjata, Sterjo Spasse, Fatos Arapi, Qamil Buxheli, Neshat Tozaj (with his latest novel "Knives" - exposing the tricks played by the Albanian Secret Police against the simple people).

In Kosovo and to a lesser degree in Macedonia and Montenegro, a modern Albanian literary movement came into being only from 1945 onwards.

The best representatives are : Esat Mekuli, whose collection of poems "For you" (Perty) was for long his finest poetic achievement; Ivzi Sulejmani, author of the great novel "The Wind and the Pillar" (Era dhe Kolona); Adem Istrefi, Rexhep Qosja etc.

# VOCABULARY

The stressed syllabi by an acute accent.

The fixed element in nouns is marked by an oblique stroke.

Plurals are not given, when in Albanian usage they are usually replaced by other turns of phrase. Forms are normally given in the order singular indefinite, singular definite, plural indefinite, plural definite.

For qualifying adjectives the masculine and feminine singular are given with an indication whether or not they take the connective article.

Since there is no infinitive form of the verb in literary Albanian, the form given in the vocabulary is the first person of the present indicative active: i.e. laj means not "to wash" but "I wash".

| | |
|---|---|
| Albania | Shqiperi-a |
| Albanian | shqip, e |
| in Albanian | shqip |
| In English | anglisht |
| good morning, good day | miredita |
| good evening | mirembrema |
| goodbye | mirupafshim |
| thank you | falemiderit |
| your health ! | gezuar ! |
| Yes | po |
| no | jo |
| Mr | zoteri, - a (-nj, - nje) |
| Mrs | zonj/e, - a (- a, - at) |
| child | femij/e, - a(- , t) |
| girl | vajz/e, - a (-a, - at) |
| boy | djal/e, i (djem, djemt) |
| woman | grua, -ja, (gra, grate) |
| man | burre, - i ( - a, - at) |
| son | bi/r - ra (- j, -jt) |
| brother | vell/a,-ai (- ezer, - eserit) |
| sister | mot/er, -ra (-ra, - rat) |
| mother | nene, -a (-a, - at) |

| | |
|---|---|
| father | at/o, -i (eter, -eterit) |
| When? | Kur ? |
| time | koh/e, - a ( - e, et) |
| hour | or/e, - a (-e, et) |
| minute | minut/e, -a (-a, -at) |
| second | skond/e, -a (-a, -at) |
| date | dat/e, -a (-a, -at) |
| timetable | orar, - i (-e, - et) |
| today | sot |
| yesterday | dje |
| the day before yesterday | pardje |
| tomorrow | pardje |
| the day after tomorrow | pasneser |
| morning | mengjes, -i (-e, - et) |
| afternoon | pasdit/e, -ja (e, - et) |
| this evening | sonte |
| this year | sirjet |
| midnight | mesnat/e, - a |
| night | nate, nata (net, netet) |
| day | dit/e, - a ( - e, et) |
| week | jav/e, - a, (-e, -et) |
| Sunday | diel, -a ( - e) |
| Monday | hen/e, - a ( - e) |
| Tuesday | mart.e, a( -e) |
| Wednesday | merkur/e, a ( -e) |
| Thursday | enjt/e, -ja (e) |
| Friday | premt/e, -ja (-e) |
| Saturday | shtun/e, - a( - e) |
| month | muaj, - i (-t) |
| January | janar, - i |
| February | shkurt, i |
| March | mars, i |
| April | prill, - i |
| May | maj, - i |
| June | qershor, oi |
| July | Korrik, - u |
| August | gusht, o i |
| September | shtator, - i |
| October | tetor, -i |
| November | nentor, - i |
| December | dhjetor, - i |

| | |
|---|---|
| year | vit, -i (-e, -et or vjet,vjetet) |
| spring | pranvere, - a |
| summer | ver.e, -a ( -a, - at) |
| autumn | vjesht.e, - a (-a, - at) |
| winter | dim/er - ri (-ra, -rat) |
| now | tani |
| always | gjithmone |
| never | kurre |
| formerly | dikur |
| late | vone |
| Where? | Ku ? |
| here | ketu |
| there | atje |
| that way | andej |
| in front of | para |
| behind | drejt |
| to the right | djathtas |
| to the left | majtas |
| near | afer |
| far | larg |
| outside | jashte |
| beside | prane |
| below | poshte |
| opposite | perballe |
| everywhere | kudo |
| north | veri |
| south | jug |
| east | lindje |
| west | perendim |
| Customs | Dogan/e, - a (-a, -at) |
| frontier | kufi, -ri (ju, - jt) |
| passport | pasaport/e, (-a, -at) |
| visa | viz/e, - a (-a, -at) |
| declare | deklaroj (deklarora, deklaruar) |
| embassy | embasad.e, -a, -at) |
| change (verb) | kembej (kembera, kembyer) |
| money | par/e, - ja (e, -et) |
| alcohol | alkool, -i (e, et) |
| Car, automobile | makin/e, -a (-a, - et) |
| direction | drejtim, -i (-e, -et) |

| | |
|---|---|
| bend | kthes/e, -a, (-a, -at) |
| junction, crossroads | kryquzimn -i (-e, -et) |
| petrol | benzin/e, -a |
| railway | kekurudh/e -a (-a, -at) |
| ticket | bilet/e, -a (-a, -at) |
| luggage | bagazh, -i (-e, -et) |
| boat | anije/e, - a (-e, -et) |
| aircraft | aeroplan, -i (-e, -et) |
| Hotel | Hotel, - i (-e, -et) |
| room | dhom/e, -a(-a, -at) |
| bed | krevat, -i (-e, -et) |
| ground floor | perdhes, -e |
| floor | kat, -i (-e, -et) |
| reception | pritj/e, -a (-e, -et) |
| wash-basin | lavaman, -i (-e, -et) |
| shower | dush -i (-e, -et) |
| bath | banj/e, -a(-a, at) |
| lavatory, toilet | nevojtor/e, -ja (e,et) |
| safe | arj/e, -a (-a, -at) |
| lift | ashensor, -i (-,t) |
| radio | radio, -ja (-t) |
| radiator | radiator, -i (-e,-et) |
| chambermaid | sherbyes/e, -ja (-e, et) |
| Restaurant | Restorant, -i (-,et) |
| eat | ha (hengra, ngren-) |
| drink (verb) | pi (piva, pire) |
| drink (noun | pij/e, -a (-e,-et) |
| menu | menu,-ja (-te) |
| waiter | kamarier, -i (-e, et) |
| waitress | kamarier/e, -ja (-e,-et) |
| food, dish | gjell/e-a,(-e,-et) |
| specialty | specialitet,-i(-e,-et) |
| bread, meal | buk/e(-e,-et) |
| breakfast | mengjes,-i(-e,-et) |
| lunch | drek/e,-a(-a,-at) |
| dinner | dark/e,-a(-a,-at) |
| European-style | allafranga |
| Oriental-style | allaturka |
| cool | fresket (-i,e) |
| hot | ngrohte (-i,e) |
| litre | liter, -ri (-ra,-rat) |

| | |
|---|---|
| pepper (pimento) | piperk/e,-a (-a,-at) |
| salt | krip/e,-a(era,-erat) |
| pepper | piper,-i |
| oil | vaj,-i (ra,-rat) |
| vinegar | uthull,-a |
| sugar | sheqer,-i |
| appetizers (with drinks) | mese,-je (-te) |
| butter | gjalpe,-i |
| cheese | djath/e,-i(era,-erat) |
| yoghurt | kos,-i |
| milk | qumesht,-i |
| wine | ver/e,-a (-a,-at) |
| water | uje,-i(-era,-erat) |
| brandy | rak, -a |
| ice | aku/ll,-lli(-j,-jt) |
| beer | arr/e,-a(-a,-at) |
| tea | caj,-i |
| coffee | kaf/e,-ja(-e,-et) |
| tobacco | duhan,-i |
| cigarette | cigar/e,-ja(-e,-et) |
| table | tavoline, -a(-a,-at) |
| plate | pjat/e,-a(-a,-at) |
| fork | piru/n, -ni (-nj, -njt) |
| knife | thik/e,-a,-at |
| spoon | lug/e, -a(-e,-et) |
| glass | got/e,-a(-a,-at) |
| bottle | shikh/e,-ja (-e,-et) |
| cup | filshan,-i |
| Post office | Post/e,-a (-a,-at) |
| name | em/er,-ri (ra,-rat) |
| address | adres/e,-a(-a, -at) |
| send | dergoj (dergora, derguar) |
| addressee | marres, -it,-i |
| sender | dergres,-i (it) |
| letter | leter,-ra (-ra,-rat) |
| postcard | kartolin/e,-a(-a,-at) |
| Feel ill | Me dhemb |
| ill | semure (i,e) |
| illness | semundj/e,-a (-e,-et) |
| doctor | mejk,-u (,-et) |
| chemist's shop | farmaci, -a(-a,-at) |

| | |
|---|---|
| prescription | recet/e,-a(-a,-at |
| medicine | ilac,-i (-e,-et) |
| ointment | melham, -i(-e,-et) |
| syrup | shurup,-i (-e,-et) |
| constipated | kaps (invar) |
| diarrhoea | diarre, -ja |
| needle, injection | gjilper/e,-a(-a,-at) |
| influenza | grip, -i |
| wound, sore | plag/e,-a(-a,-at) |
| hospital | spital,-i (-e,et) |
| intestines | sorr/e,-a(-e,-et) |
| blood | gjak,-ju(-qu,qet) |
| tooth | dhemb,-i (e,-et) |
| dentist | dentist,-i (-e,-et) |
| buy | blej (blera,blere) |
| shop | dyqan,-i (-e, -et) |
| church | kish/e,-i (-e,-et) |
| monastery | manastir, -a (-a,-at) |
| abby | abaci, -a (-te) |
| capital | kryeqytet, -i (-e, -et) |
| quarter, district | lagje, -a (-e, -et) |
| village | fshat, -t (-ra,-rat) |
| citadel | kals, -ja (-te) |
| fortress | fortese, -a (-a, -at) |
| tower, keep | kull/e,-a (-a,-lt) |
| museum | muze, -u (-te) |
| exhibition | krye, kreu (krere, kreret) |
| match | ndeshj/e,-a(-e,-et) |
| | |
| one | nje |
| two | dy |
| three | tre, tri |
| four | kater |
| five | pese |
| six | gjashte |
| seven | shtate |
| eight | tete |
| nine | nente |
| ten | dhjete |

## Index to Town Guides

| Town | Pge |
|---|---|
| *Berat* | *98* |
| *Durres* | *52* |
| *Elbasan* | *113* |
| *Fier* | *59* |
| *Gjirokastra* | *68* |
| *Kanina* | *92* |
| *Kavaja* | *55* |
| *Korce* | *118* |
| *Kruja* | *44* |
| *Kukes* | *132* |
| *Lezha* | *40* |
| *Lukova* | *88* |
| *Lushnja* | *57* |
| *Maliq* | *118* |
| *Permet* | *124* |
| *Peshkopia* | *139* |
| *Pogradec* | *116* |
| *Saranda* | *78* |
| *Shkodra* | *34* |
| *Tepelena* | *66* |
| *Tirana* | *104* |
| *Tropoja* | *131* |
| *Valbona* | *129* |
| *Vlora* | *93* |

*NOTES*

*NOTES*

*NOTES*

*NOTES*

*NOTES*

*NOTES*

*NOTES*

*NOTES*